Reading J.Z. Smith

Reading J.Z. Smith

Interviews and Essay

Edited by
WILLI BRAUN
RUSSELL T. McCUTCHEON

OXFORD
UNIVERSITY PRESS

Oxford University Press is a department of the University of Oxford. It furthers
the University's objective of excellence in research, scholarship, and education
by publishing worldwide. Oxford is a registered trade mark of Oxford University
Press in the UK and certain other countries.

Published in the United States of America by Oxford University Press
198 Madison Avenue, New York, NY 10016, United States of America.

© Oxford University Press 2018

All rights reserved. No part of this publication may be reproduced, stored in
a retrieval system, or transmitted, in any form or by any means, without the
prior permission in writing of Oxford University Press, or as expressly permitted
by law, by license, or under terms agreed with the appropriate reproduction
rights organization. Inquiries concerning reproduction outside the scope of the
above should be sent to the Rights Department, Oxford University Press, at the
address above.

You must not circulate this work in any other form
and you must impose this same condition on any acquirer.

Library of Congress Cataloging-in-Publication Data
Names: Braun, Willi, 1954– editor. | McCutcheon, Russell T. editor.
Title: Reading J.Z. Smith : Interviews & Essay /
Edited by Willi Braun and Russell T. McCutcheon.
Description: New York : Oxford University Press, 2018. |
Includes bibliographical references and index.
Identifiers: LCCN 2018016586 (print) | LCCN 2018022487 (ebook) |
ISBN 9780190879099 (updf) | ISBN 9780190879105 (epub) |
ISBN 9780190879082 (cloth)
Subjects: LCSH: Smith, Jonathan Z.—Interviews. |
Religion historians—United States—Interviews. | Religion.
Classification: LCC BL43.S645 (ebook) | LCC BL43.S645 A5 2018 (print) |
DDC 200.92—dc23
LC record available at https://lccn.loc.gov/2018016586

Contents

Introduction vii

Interviews

The Chicago Maroon: Interview with Jonathan Z. Smith (2008) 3

The American Scholars of Religion Video Project: Interview with
 Jonathan Z. Smith (1999) 29

*Asdiwal: Revue genevoise d'anthropologie et d'histoire des
 religions*: Interview with Jonathan Z. Smith (2010) 45

The Devil in Mr. Smith: A Conversation with Jonathan Z. Smith
 (2012) 62

The Dean's Craft of Teaching Seminar (2013) 85

Essay

Reading Religion: A Life in Learning (2010) 111

Index 129

"I don't want to train anybody for something. I really don't like that role—I play it but I don't like it. I really want to enable interesting gossip."

– JONATHAN Z. SMITH (1938–2017)

Introduction

Willi Braun and Russell T. McCutcheon

As with all readers, we each first met Jonathan Z. Smith (1938–2017) as a text. One of us came across Smith's earlier books in graduate school because of his and Smith's shared interests in Christian origins, and the other, working well outside that field, because the first told him he should be reading Smith—not necessarily for what he was studying (which Smith unashamedly and routinely refers to as data), but, instead, for what he did with it. Take, for example, the way much of Smith's work insists on and illustrates how to go about comparing two things with respect to a third. According to him, it is this kind of comparison that also goes beyond merely observing patterns of similarity and difference between things, such as religions, and that goes beyond comparison for the sake of establishing something as exceptional, even unique and thus incomparable, as has often been the case in the study of religions. Rather, Smith's comparison of two things "with respect" to a third (e.g., comparing two stones in light of their weight) becomes in his work a robust theory of comparison that asks "the 'how' and 'why' and, above all, the 'so what' of comparison" (*Imagining Religion*).[1] The "why" and "so what" are especially important, because they point to none other than the scholar's own questions and interests—that's the one who decided that, of all the ways to compare them, it was the weight of the stones that was worth observing. So, comparing finally is not about the similarity or difference of the things compared, but is instead in the service of some intellectual interests and curiosities of the scholar. (Smith's 1990 book on the study of early Christianities,

---

1. Jonathan Z. Smith. (1982). *Imagining Religion: From Babylon to Jonestown*. Chicago: University of Chicago Press, 35.

Drudgery Divine, also nicely makes the operations of a properly academic comparison explicit.)[2] Reading Smith in grad school was therefore a lesson, for each of us, in how to become a self-conscious scholar, in how to own the fact that some mundane thing in the world struck us (and ideally others, such that you had some colleagues and conversation partners) as worth studying and talking about. It was therefore a lesson, again for each of us, in theorizing, that is, in choosing and positioning the mere stuff that we observed, items among the wide range of human doings, *into* data—into an, as he might phrase it, *exempli gratia* (Latin: for the sake of example), thereby making clear that the object stood out not of its own accord but, rather, because it served *our* purposes and satisfied *our* curiosities. (The word "data" is therefore a handy reminder for the active role that observers play in all this—i.e., because of the constitutive role that we, as scholars, play, none of us studies merely found objects.)

Now this was in the late 1980s, when his *Imagining Religion* was still a relatively new collection of essays and thus had not yet reached the point of being virtually canonical in the field. And his introductory claim there—"*there is no data for religion*. Religion is solely the creation of the scholar's study. It is created for the scholar's analytic purposes by his imaginative acts of comparison and generalization. Religion has no independent existence apart from the academy" (xi)—had yet to seep throughout the field. But by now it has. It is now a line that's been cited so many times as to become a commonplace rather than the provocation that we think Smith intended. But that's what happens in all social formations, across their lifetime. Academic disciplines are no different. With their success, revolutions get normalized, and what were once outliers can get canonized, making them suitable targets for the iconoclasts who come after them, seeking a revolution (and thus influence) of their own.

Smith's work in the study of religion is no different. For today we find a younger generation, trained by the people who were trained by the people who in some cases might have trained with people of Smith's generation (he defended his own dissertation, "The Glory, Jest and Riddle: James George Frazer and *The Golden Bough*," at Yale in 1969)—a generation who, in taking them for granted, now question

---

2. Jonathan Z. Smith. (1990). *Drudgery Divine: On the Comparison of Early Christianities and the Religions of Late Antiquity.* Chicago: University of Chicago Press.

the gains that his work helped the field to achieve. We recognize that his rigorous attention to scholars and how their interests actively shape the field is a challenge that can be a little unnerving. After all, the above-cited passage from *Imagining Religion* went on to say (in a portion that few quote today) that "the student of religion . . . must be relentlessly self-conscious. Indeed, this self-consciousness constitutes his primary expertise, his foremost object of study" (xi). Not all are up to the challenge, it seems; for despite Smith's foundational requirement for the student of religion, the field has, for some, turned into one where we somehow already know that things just are religious. And thus we often find ourselves debating how best to study those self-evidently religious things, especially in ways that do not undermine the way the people we study already talk about their own worlds. But wait: it has not *turned* into that sort of field, but, we would suggest, *returned* to that sort of field, since much of Smith's work can be understood as a reaction to that of his once-senior University of Chicago colleague, Mircea Eliade (1907–1986). For whereas Eliade was (and still is) famously known for asserting a uniqueness to religion, simply recognized by the careful interpreter, a camouflaged essence that demanded an equally unique method for its adequate study, Smith's essays illustrate just how mundane those things we call religion really are—until, that is, a disciplined scholar, using commonplace tools but armed with a specific sort of curiosity, arrives on the scene and, quite literally, *makes something of it all*. It is therefore with some irony, at least to us, that some recent critics of Smith seem to be advocating for the very position against which he has worked so hard throughout his long career, a position we see in those more recent approaches that are devoted to such things as religion on the ground, lived religion, and material religion. For from these subfields yet other scholars are often criticized for obscuring the local, the indigenous, and the authentic by not letting people speak for themselves—as if human beings spontaneously walk around and, in some unprovoked manner, talk about their meanings and motivations. Failing, in our estimation, to heed Smith's advice concerning relentless self-consciousness, some among this newer generation seem intent not just on identifying scholarly interests (and this is where they acknowledge their indebtedness to Smith) but, reversing his work, also in criticizing them as inappropriately foisted onto the people whom they study, suppressing their own unique voices, in what seems to be the hope that a self-evident

Other will emerge once the layers of their academic interpretations and explanations are removed.

This reaction, this return to authenticity strikes us as flying in the face of the past thirty years of work across the liberal arts, especially in such fields as anthropology and literary criticism, but also in such fields as race and gender studies—work in which scholars have argued (persuasively, in our estimation) that, for example, there is no such thing as culture floating out there in the world (or lurking in people's heads). Instead, it is a creation of an observer in a situation, the one who names and delimits, the one who classifies and organizes the world, making the judgment call on where this thing called, for instance, French culture starts and ends. (Its fabricated status hardly makes it unreal, of course—ask a modern Muslim woman in France who is contested over covering her head if efforts to normalize one notion of Frenchness are without practical effects.) We think here of the classic photo on the cover of Jim Clifford's and George Marcus's once-influential collection of essays, *Writing Culture: The Poetics and Politics of Ethnography* (1986):[3] the ethnographer, seated on a small woven veranda, immersed in a fieldwork setting, his research subject (presumably) seated behind him, unengaged, while he writes in a notebook. The point? Although human subjects are innovative and creative, the cultures in which they are thought to live and act are created in that notebook (by no less creative and innovative anthropologists), in response to the queries of observers who arrive on the scene curious as to why their research subjects do this or that—translation: curious as to why others' actions deviate from how they themselves think the world works. For what else is curiosity but the result of an intellectually (maybe even socially) jarring moment when the world fails to work as you had anticipated that it might? Or that it should. Or maybe even as it ought. (Curiosity is therefore linked to juxtaposition.)

So the turn that we see across a variety of fields, over the past two generations or so, was something that also took place in the study of religion thanks to Smith's work (among the work of others) on religion, myth, ritual, canon, sacrifice, and so forth, all done with a careful eye toward the need to classify and the implications of those classifications. But we'd be naïve to think that the position against which he and others

---

3. James Clifford and George E. Marcus. (1986). *Writing Culture: The Poetics and Politics of Ethnography*. Berkeley: University of California Press.

argued—a position that saw scholarly theories as a nonessential nuisance—would bow out gracefully. Instead, as noted above, the drive to see the world as already animated and thus inherently meaningful, well before we arrive on the scene with our questions and our notebooks, is strong and, in our reading, is back. (Come to think of it, maybe that very drive is what we should be studying!)

All of this amounts, as least as we see things, to a compelling and timely reason for the present little volume. Especially for those not yet acquainted with the debates into which Smith weighed since the 1970s, as well as for those who have yet to work through his essays (and yes, he is an essayist: not an insignificant fact, as will become apparent), these transcriptions of interviews that he did over the years nicely set the table—often in provocative, pithy, and sometimes even humorous ways—for discussions on issues still close to the heart of this field. But because these are interviews, the fact of a questioner is evident (though sometimes more hidden than you would think), making the situation of exchange, translation, interpretation, disagreement, compromise, convergence, and advance all the more apparent. For what we have here are not proclamations but, instead, replies that tell us as much about the one doing the interviewing as the one answering the questions—all of which nicely illustrates the critical turn we associate with Smith's work. So we feel that these interviews are likely the best place to begin to think through his project, to understand it, and to begin to assess its implications for where this field might go in the coming decades. For a monograph or an essay disguises the conversation of which it is but one part; sure, there are footnotes and references, but only careful readers will keep in mind that any text is always an explicit response to something that went before—either in agreement or not. Interviews prevent us from overlooking this.

But, as we noted in our opening line, because we each were introduced to Smith's work through text, but also because we were each lucky enough to get to know him in person—mostly through conferences, where he would sit, listening intently to a presentation, with his hands and head atop that tree limb of a cane that he used—we tend to think that, although transcriptions of interviews certainly are text, they nonetheless suggest something of the dynamic, thinking-on-his feet style that we came to appreciate about Smith. For, much as with the reason one of us told the other to read him, the point is not with where the answer takes him, but with the process by which he gets there. To put it another way, keep in mind how often the question itself, along with the questioner's assumptions, becomes the thing that Smith examines in his reply. And it's this combined self-consciousness when it comes to his approach to a problem and also the "making it up as you go"—not freewheeling, of course, since there is a theory of signification (how we go about making meaning rather than passively recognizing it when we see it in the wild) that he's working with—that we find so nicely represented in these interviews.

Before concluding, a note on the transcriptions: while more information about the interviews is provided at the opening of each, the transcriptions for this collection (including the final, previously unpublished essay by Smith, which was originally presented as the American Academy of Religion's Lifetime of Learning Address, in 2010) were made by Andie Alexander, a graduate of the University of Alabama's Department of Religious Studies who is now enrolled in Emory University's PhD program. After the editors checked and then double-checked her transcriptions against the original (which, in some cases, were relatively unknown audio or video files), they were smoothed out, somewhat, by removing the inevitable verbal cues that we each use when speaking off the cuff (we refer to the "errs" and "ahhs"). Although these cues were likely necessary, we regret removing them, however, since for us they signify the thinking that was taking place somewhere offstage, and thus the work required for that thinking and the exchange taking place in a conversation. Sources for the originals from which these transcriptions were made are publicly available (and noted in each chapter; and our appreciation goes to all of our sources for their kind permission to use each interview here), so we would encourage readers to find them, to listen and watch for themselves, so as not to mistake what follows as proclamations, but, instead, to bear in mind the situation and both its structure (the questions) and novelty (the answers).

Finally, editorial notes appear throughout the work, intended to assist readers for whom some of the following may be new, either to provide additional information on an item discussed in the interview or to suggest places in Smith's body of work where interested readers can find lengthier and more formal discussions of a topic mentioned in here.

Before closing, we would like to thank Jonathan himself, who passed away on December 30, 2017, for his permission to tackle this project and his assistance with it (such as his agreement to include the final essay). It began several years ago and took longer to complete than we had anticipated. Although we regret that he will not see this little volume, we are grateful that, in hindsight, it provided us with additional opportunities to correspond with him and to meet with him in Chicago, to discuss the project along with a host of other issues that interested him (from the state of the field to the state of the garden outside his Hyde Park graystone, a short walk from his onetime office at the University of Chicago). We would also like to thank his wife, Elaine, who was always a gracious host and willing to convey our email messages to him, which were always sent to her (because, as will become clear in the following, he was not a computer user). And finally, with Jonathan's family in mind, we make note of the addendum that Jonathan signed that ensures that all author's royalties from the sale of this volume will, now, go directly to his estate.

We hope that readers familiar with him or his work find something of value in these interviews and essay and that those who are new to it and who never had the good fortune either to meet him or hear him deliver a conference paper in his slow and steady style, will become intrigued enough to find any of his many published essays, chapters, and replies. For, in our experience, any time invested in his work will definitely repay itself.

Interviews

The Chicago Maroon

INTERVIEW WITH JONATHAN Z. SMITH (2008)

A word of advice for anyone hoping to contact Jonathan Zittell Smith before he returns to campus next fall: Use the mail slot. The religious studies professor—better known as J.Z.—doesn't pick up the phone and has never "seen the Internet." In a two-hour interview, Smith weighed in on chain smoking, dead religions, and the Babylonian Talmud.

SUPRIYA SINHABABU: I've interviewed a fair number of people, but you are by far the most difficult I've ever had to contact. Why is that?

JONATHAN Z. SMITH: Well, I despise the telephone. That's probably why. I don't like it. I'll reveal my age, but I don't like the notion [that] for a nickel . . . anyone could get a hold of me any time they want. I think the cell phone is an absolute abomination. I don't understand people really needing to take a telephone with them. I have one in the kitchen, and it has an answering machine, and I pay no attention whatsoever.

SUPRIYA SINHABABU: How about e-mail?

JONATHAN Z. SMITH: I've never used a computer.

SUPRIYA SINHABABU: Never?

JONATHAN Z. SMITH: No.

SUPRIYA SINHABABU: So do you typewrite all your papers?

JONATHAN Z. SMITH: Yup. Or handwrite them. I just gave a 90-page paper in California—just came back. I had to get an honorary degree in Canada and take a flight from Toronto to Los Angeles, which I do not recommend. Especially if you chain-smoke, it's not a good trip. But my son talked me into the patch. My God it works! My wife said she could stand me, and usually on the airline she can't at all. She said I was relaxed. I didn't think so, but that's what she said. I had fantasies of cigarettes all the way to California. But she thought I was relaxed, so she said, "Maybe you should always wear one!" She wouldn't let me smoke with it on. But no, that one I gave with a handwritten paper.

No, I take Marx very seriously, I think [the computer] alienates the worker from his production—I do not understand. With a typewriter, I hit a key, and it goes bam. I understand that: I made that letter happen. Now, I then got one of these Smith-Corona things that has a little window. Allegedly you can delete things and so on. And that already bothered me because, number one, it's mysterious, but number two, it doesn't have a bell at the end of the line. And all my life I've said, "Gee, that was a good day. I had a 30-bell day" or "I had an 80-bell day," and Elaine would say, "How's it coming?," and I'd say, "Three more bells!" So first I thought I'd get a hotel bell, but I also don't like the idea that it decides when a word stops. And I like to put a hyphen in and decide myself where the word stops. Because to me it makes a big difference, especially when reading something aloud. I could lose a whole syllable with this stupid thing. So I haven't graduated past that, and now my Smith-Corona broke down, so I'm very happy because now I do everything by hand again. Because then it's mine!

SUPRIYA SINHABABU: What got you interested in the religions that you study?

JONATHAN Z. SMITH: Because they're funny. They're interesting in and of themselves. They relate to the world in which I live, but it's like a fun house mirror: something's off. It's not quite the world I live in, yet it's recognizable. So that gap interested me. And so I specialized in religions that are dead, which has the great advantage that nobody talks back. No one says, "That's not what I heard last Sunday!" Everybody's dead. And I like that. Now, I sometimes have to deal with religions that keep going. And they're more problematic because then you deal with people who believe things. They also find their own beliefs puzzling or challenging or interesting—they're almost synonyms. So they have not only their beliefs, but their interpretations of those beliefs. And I have my interpretations of their beliefs. Sometimes we can sit like this and negotiate it. Other times it's in a book or transcript. And then in a third sense you have to run back and forth. You have to represent both sides of the conversation as you try to figure out what it's all about. You get good at doing that with dead people because you'll never hear from them because you have to do it all the time.

And that's what a historian does. They run back and forth to make both sides of a conversation happen. I also think that whether you like it or you don't like it, [religion's] been a part of the world, and remains a part of the world that has a lot to do with what people do. And so I think if you think it's a worthwhile task to try to understand other people, then you probably haven't given up on trying to understand yourself. Then you would call religion a peril. We see bad results from countries or other countries' religions. But you don't have to go to war over it, you could just piss somebody off. So it's a question of a world that, whether an individual sees themselves as religious, there is still enough embedded in the culture in which they live [that], to some degree, the eyeglasses through which they look at the world are shaped by those religions.

I started off originally in grass breeding.[1] That was what I wanted to do with my life. I went to a farm, because . . . if you're a city boy going [to] an agricultural school, which is free, you have to prove that you can stand in cow shit, so they send you to a barn for a while. I did that, and I loved it. It still remains to this day the best thing I ever did in my life. But it was a bad time in Cornell's history. They would let you take no liberal arts courses: It was all part of the agriculture, which was my program. And for my interests I had a program called elementary corn development. And I don't know if you've ever seen corn roots but they're only about this big. So to think there were people intermediate and advanced ahead of me—I mean I had lots of other interests! So I said, "What about history, philosophy, things like that?" and they said, "Well, you're at an agricultural school which is free. If you went to Cornell University, then of course. . . ." So I said, "What if I paid a little money?" and they said no. So I went to the headmaster of the high school and told him what had happened. He said, "You're such a stubborn son of a bitch. It probably would have taken you two years to realize agriculture wasn't for you. But that's good, you'll go to Haverford; they'll figure you out there." So that's what I did. He made a phone call—in the old days, there was the old-boy network that everyone is so worried about. So I never applied to college, because Cornell just took me as a junior, and Haverford got a phone call, so I went.

---

1. Ed. Note: See Jonathan Z. Smith, "When the Chips Are Down," in Smith, *Relating Religion: Essays in the Study of Religion* (Chicago: University of Chicago Press, 2004), 1–2, 19–20.

And the first day there I met this remarkable man in the philosophy department, Mark Foss, and I think largely, education is an "Oh, when I grow [up] I'd like to be like this" sort of affair. This was a guy—wow. So I became a philosophy major. I met him by accident. I was so enthralled. I went to this one place in the library that looked like the only place you could smoke. There were all these comfortable chairs. Turns out it was a shrine where Quaker philosophers would study. And if there was one place where no one had ever smoked before, that was it. So there I was, happy as could be. There were these armchairs that extended out six feet, and you could sit and put your legs up. But anyway, there I was. Then a man came in. Then some other students came in, and there was supposed to be a senior philosophy seminar on Hegel's *Phenomenology of Mind*. And from Marx I had read some Hegel, not that one, but I knew some vocabulary. And I was absolutely enthralled by his way of talking. So that afternoon I became a philosophy major. And then when it got time to go to graduate school, I asked another philosophy professor—when I got interested in a problem that people were worried about for much of the earlier 20th century, how myth and philosophy interrelate. Mostly philosophers yell at myths; nonetheless, if you read them carefully, you'll see how much they've been appropriated. So I thought I would like to do that, but not with Greek myth. And so I went to another philosophy professor—Mark had retired by then—and I said where can I go to study Greek myths. He said, "Why don't you go to Yale Divinity School and study the New Testament, it's the biggest piece of Greek myth that's still around."

SUPRIYA SINHABABU: [Laughs]

JONATHAN Z. SMITH: See, you're smarter than I am. I didn't catch it as a joke. So I went to Yale Divinity School to study the New Testament, and here I am. But I still don't know that there's a place where you could get a degree in such a subject. You might persuade a classics department. You might persuade a history of art department. You'd really have to talk a blue streak to do it. And I think nowadays you'd probably have to go construct your own major in college, because they're very unimaginative. I don't know why I said they—we're all very unimaginative. Philosophy was no good for me after college because it was in the height of its analytic phase, and you certainly weren't going to go study mythology with these guys. They're arguing about whether what I just said made any sense, let alone blue, green people climbing in trees or something; it's not for them. So I knew I couldn't go on unless I radically changed what I thought I was doing. So then I've taught religion ever since. Some say peculiarly, but nonetheless I've taught it.

Usually something on one of the old religions. Usually something on the Bible, because that's what a lot of people like to talk about. And usually something on the anthropology of religion, I guess you'd call it. I tried always to be comparative.[2] We never look at one thing; we always look at more than one thing. Even years ago when I used to teach a course, Bibles in Western Civ, which was then a Western Civ requirement, for three quarters I would do the Hebrew Bible, the New Testament, the Koran, and the Book of Mormon as "the Bibles of the West." Because it doesn't have just one Bible, it has a bunch of Bibles, and we might as well take a look at them. Even that makes it simpler than it is, because it depends on whose New Testament you look at, whether it has 24 books, 27 books, or 38 books, and so on. I think that's what got me interested in grass, how many kinds of grass there are. I'm fascinated by how many kinds of religions there are, how many kinds of Bibles there are. Linnaeus gave us a way of talking about the diversity of grasses. I don't think looking at their sex organs is the most interesting way, but nonetheless he gave us a way of talking. Some types of grass, if you've dealt with them, have very small little organs. You have to use a tiny brush that has one camel's hair in it, and you have to go back and forth. But two, two will damage it already, it's that strong. I still have one brush left. I haven't used it for years. I keep it to remember. I could have spent my life with a binocular microscope going like this: [Smith makes brushstrokes in the air]. Good to remember.

---

2. Ed. Note: Smith speaks of comparison, and the inseparable idea of taxonomy or classification, as among his "persistent preoccupations." See "When the Chips Are Down," in Smith, *Relating Religion*, 19–25. He himself identifies his most "programmatic essays" on comparison as "*Adde Parvum Parvo Magnus Acervus Erit*," *History of Religions* 11 (1971), 67–90, reprinted in Smith, *Map Is Not Territory: Studies in the History of Religions* (Leiden: Brill, 1978), 240–64; "In Comparison a Magic Dwells," in Smith, *Imagining Religion: From Babylon to Jonestown* (Chicago: University of Chicago Press, 1982), 19–35; *Drudgery Divine: On the Comparison of Early Christianities and the Religions of Late Antiquity* (London: School of Oriental and African Studies; Chicago: University of Chicago Press, 1990), especially chapter 2: "On Comparison": "Epilogue: The 'End' of Comparison," in K. C. Patton and B. C. Ray, eds., *A Magic Still Dwells: Comparative Religion in the Postmodern Age* (Berkeley: University of California Press, 2000), 237–41; "Acknowledgements: Morphology and History in Mircea Eliade's *Patterns in Comparative Religions* (1949–1999), part I, The Work and Its Contexts," *History of Religions* 39 (2000), 315–31; "Acknowledgements: Morphology and History in Mircea Eliade's *Patterns in Comparative Religions* (1949–1999), part II, The Work and Its Contexts," *History of Religions* 39 (2000), 332–51, reprinted in Smith, *Relating Religion*, 61–100.

SUPRIYA SINHABABU: Do you still do that anymore?

JONATHAN Z. SMITH: No, I don't. I do fool around in the garden, and grow certain grasses, that grow wild around here, that I've transplanted. This new popularity of ornamental grasses—they're basically grasses that have a hard time surviving, because they're so ornamental. I have ordinary grass, common, but I like its shape, so I have about eight kinds.

SUPRIYA SINHABABU: You mentioned that your teaching style is peculiar. Can you describe what you mean by that?

JONATHAN Z. SMITH: Oh, I don't know. Well, first of all, given the range of religions I teach, the issue of where I stand in relation to them is moot. And most people who teach religion have a clear relationship with the religions. I cannot. Obviously, most of them are dead. I would get in trouble with the ASPCA [American Society for the Prevention of Cruelty to Animals] if I sacrificed a bull ox to Zeus. I have a friend, who recently died, but he actually decided to show kids what a sacrifice looks like, so he sacrificed a lamb at Easter time.[3] "We talk about it so much—here's what it looks like!" Half the class puked, half the class had angry letters from mommy and daddy. But he did demonstrate that it's not just a metaphor. It's a messy and not altogether pleasant process. Since [then] we've converted it entirely into an economic question. I ask students the meaning of sacrifice, and they always start talking about "mommy and daddy sacrificing so I could go to college." We've been at war for four years, and I haven't heard one person yet say some soldiers sacrificed themselves. That language is gone. It's entirely economic. One kid whose name I sent to the Development Office said sacrifice was [not] joining a golf club for the four years that he was here, so he would have money to go to Europe when he graduated. I thought Development ought to keep an eye on that kid. I rarely do that, but I turned him in. That's just his notion, but it's the same idea—it's economic: "I give up something now to get a better thing in the future." Well that's a shitty theory of sacrifice. But that's the kind of thing I try to do, I try to make students answer questions, and not in class, but in writing.

---

3. Ed. Note: Smith is here referring to a well-known story told about Gary Lease (d. 2008), the longtime chair of the History of Consciousness Program (at the University of California, Santa Cruz), who once incorporated an actual sacrifice into his course, which, as Lease told the story, elicited just the reaction Smith describes.

On the whole I don't teach seminars. I used to teach a lot of seminars. It's a young man's game. Some people like [University of Chicago Classics professor James] Redfield can keep it up. I can't. It's very tiring. To really keep track of what everybody's saying is like a computer dating service—"You should really talk to him," or "Come on, stop talking!"—it's like conducting an orchestra. And I can't do it any longer. So I mostly talk. And I let them talk back in writing basically. And sometimes I'll identify who asked something—it depends on how many people are in the room. If there's 20, I'll identify them. If there's 80, I won't. I try, I suppose, very hard. Someone once said religion is a topic you have to un-teach before you teach, because in some sense, everybody comes in with an idea in their head, so they're obviously sure that they know something about it. Your job is to suggest, without being incredibly in their face, that they don't. So you have to take it apart, respectfully, but nonetheless take it apart. And sometimes you try juxtaposing it to something, you sometimes try asking an awful long question about it, sometimes you play dumb. Sometimes you do some history, say, "You know, it wasn't always like you just said," and there's a reason behind why you're saying what you're saying, because something happened that caused people to talk like that. No one until Charles Darwin ever knew the Bible had no errors. No one in the history of Christianity has ever claimed . . . that the Bible had no errors, so why suddenly did they have to announce the Bible had no errors, at the beginning of the 20th century? It's not an internal religious movement; it's what they perceive as an external threat. Of course after that you drop the second shoe, which is, the sentence continues: "It's only an error in the original autograph." Well, fat chance you and I are ever going to see that one! And fat chance there ever was one, incidentally. The whole damn thing, written down in the same handwriting, all at once? No way. So you ask questions. That's what you do. And most religions that are interesting spend a lot of time asking questions.

The difference I think is when religion is left alone to ask questions; they can actually be far more daring than I can be in a classroom. And usually people who ask questions are fairly comfortable with their religion. They ask the craziest—I mean I wouldn't dare ask some of these questions. But they're never going to leave, because the answer to that question—that's who they are, and they just want to find out more about it. And if it leads them to things that make them say, "My God, yuck," they're still not going to say, "So, tomorrow I'm going to join some other group." Whereas when you deal with a mixed audience, when you deal with somebody else's faith, it gets tricky.

I loved teaching Self, Culture, and Society. It was, I think, my favorite teaching I've done here. And I would come in the winter quarter when they did religion, with Durkheim, Lévi-Strauss, all those good people. And one year we read a book about education by Derek Bok and another former president of another university, called something like *The Shape of the River*,[4] and it was an argument basically for the educational requirement for diversity. It was the book the University of Michigan used before the Supreme Court to make its argument about what Republicans like to call quotas. They're targets. A quota means you have to reach it. A target means you try, and there's a big difference, and they know damn well there's a big difference—anyway, that's neither here nor there. It's remarkable because since they were the president of Princeton and the president of Harvard, they got access to everybody in the business and they got access to everybody's files. And so they were able to give us longitudinal surveys of attitudes over a 20-, 30-year period. Alumni associations have polls, Harvard has a continual poll that they bother people with until they die. Some other places do the same thing. And they tried to summarize—and I was fascinated by a discrepancy, it seemed to me, in two questions. They said, "Do you think it is important to go to school with people of other cultures?" And I don't care what population you were looking at, the answer was always in the high nineties. Old, young, black, white, rich, poor—not so poor, for the surveys these places were doing—but still, everyone said, "Yes, it's important educationally to go to school with someone from different cultures."

But 150 pages later, they said, "Do you think it's important to go to school with someone of different beliefs?" Thirty-eight percent was the highest "yes" on that one. I looked at that. I said, "You know, I don't consider my classroom a zoo where I have to have a specimen of every animal. So clearly what I want is I want people from different places because they bring with them different beliefs. So what the hell is the difference between those two?" As interviewers sometimes do, they reword the same question and ask it. I asked Bok, whom I know, and he

---

4. Ed. Note: William Bowen and Derek Bok, *The Shape of the River: Long-Term Consequences of Considering Race in College and University Admissions* (Princeton, NJ: Princeton University Press, 1998).

said, "No, no, that wasn't it at all." He hadn't noticed the discrepancy. Well I said, "You're no god-damn use, I'll ask my students." They're the ones who presumably fill out things like this, so I asked them. And they thought I was crazy to think there was a contradiction. First of all, for them the word belief means only religious. I'd never quite realized this before. They don't have beliefs about science, or beliefs about Obama or beliefs about *War and Peace*. They only have beliefs about religion. If you say, "what do you think about . . . ," that's not beliefs! So somehow beliefs isn't about thinking about, first of all; that's the first thing I learned from my students.

Secondly, though we had read Clifford Geertz's arguments, which tell you that culture, science, everything is a matter of belief, they obviously didn't believe him. And that pissed me off, because I'd just given out some As for their reading of Clifford Geertz. And now they're telling me religion is the only thing you could believe in. All right. Now I'm beginning to catch on, aha. Well if they all read it that way, yeah I guess I see, but still. . . . Didn't they know different beliefs were going to come with all these different cultures, even if it's religion? I thought it was fascinating and horrifying—the students weren't horrifying but it was. . . . If there was someone from some place else, if there was someone from India, I could go to their house, I could like their food, I could like the samosas and go home. Or I could go to an ethnic fair and enjoy all the different—and that's a zoo!—all the different dances, foods, costumes, and all of that, and I go home. If I like someone else's religion, I have to leave and convert. I can't go home. And I listened to that, and I thought, "My God. Your choice is to be a tourist or to be a convert, there's nothing in between." There's a whole world in between! You don't have to run fast through a museum from Greek art through French impressionism, watching your clock because you have to go to a natural history museum in a couple hours. You don't have to do that. There're other things you could do. You could slow down a little bit. But you also don't have to become an apostle—there's a lot of room in between. And that really got me all reanimated about this business. I was quite struck—and I suspect they were telling me much the same things from the minds of the [surveyed] people. That explains the gap.

I thought that was quite amazing. So the question is, how can you look, like you look at a museum at something, look at it, without having to run to something else right away, but without saying—I've seen very few paintings where I'd like to live in what I see, but it doesn't stop you from looking at them for a while, trying to figure out, "What the hell's going on here, how did they do that?" You know, all the questions you ask yourself. The same kind of thing should somehow happen in the world of beliefs, even religious beliefs.

SUPRIYA SINHABABU: So do you consider yourself one of those people who's in-between?

JONATHAN Z. SMITH: Oh, I would hope so. In between is where you always are. In between is where you always are. If you want one word from me, I'm a translator. That's what I do. I translate in both directions. But what you have to remember is, it's like the original autograph, there's no original in this business. So, I'm translating other folks' translations of who they think they are or what some figure said, or for that matter, I'm translating the translation of the figure who said it. And so, you're always in the middle, because translation's always in the middle. It can't impose its language on someone else's language. On the other hand, if it just repeats the other person's language, it ain't translated. I have colleagues in the religion business who think that's what we ought to do. We ought to repeat their language. We ought to get them to sign off on our version of their language. Nonsense! Translation changes things, there's no doubt about it. I can't imagine any author has been fully satisfied with a translation of their work, even if they translated it themselves. So if I can't get the author to sign off on their own translation, why the hell—and who am I going to ask?

There's an example, of a great scholar, also named Smith—Wilfred Cantwell Smith, just died a couple years ago—[for whom] that was his fundamental principle. His specialty was particularly in Islam, and he held that if he said something about Islam, they had to sign off on it. And I said, "Wilfred, the difference between you and me is that I'm at Chicago and you're at Harvard. You're rich, I'm poor. Who are you calling up? My God, what a phone bill! I mean, you're calling up the entire Muslim world, and asking what they think of your sentence? Because if not, I want to know how you picked out the person you asked. And I suspect you picked him out because he talks just like you! And then you're asking a mirror, 'How do I look today?'" I mean, it's a crazy idea. Call up the whole world and ask them, "What do you think about what I was about to say? Every sentence?" I mean good lord, what a bill. I think even with the cell phones, I see all the ads say "unlimited"—I don't think they had that in mind. So no. Now, there are some self-appointed loudmouths who say "unless I approve of what you say"—but who the hell appointed them? So, you know, with Wendy Doniger you get in trouble with the self-appointed guardians, or something or other. But that's just . . . you get in trouble anyway. It's a pissed-off believer or a pissed-off parent. You get in trouble anyway in this business. Sooner or later, you do something someone's not going to like. Because their son or daughter translated what you said. And then they translated hearing the son or the daughter. And so it's the same issue. It's the glory and the problem of speech.

But it would be terrible if we did everything in the unambiguous world of mathematics. Here's a speech designed not to have any of these problems, to be international, to have no ambiguity of any of that. I mean it has its uses, but what an awful way to go around all day. I can't imagine. It would be a very odd conversation. I'm sure we wouldn't laugh once. They're very funny people, mathematicians, but always when they stop being mathematicians they're funny. I guess they have to be, having spent all day talking like that.

SUPRIYA SINHABABU: I know one of the people you've criticized is Joseph Campbell. What's it like to take on big fish like that?

JONATHAN Z. SMITH: He's a good friend, so that makes it easier in a way. He could drink like a fish. He could recite *Ulysses* and *Finnegan's Wake* in a fake drawl for hours. Of course, who knew if he was right or wrong half the time, but nonetheless he could do it. And since he wrote the skeletal key to *Finnegan's Wake* I presume he probably does in fact know it. But every now and then he'd come to a passage that I love that would come out as far as I can recall—of course I had had a few drinks too—but it came out letter-perfect.

Joe makes it all easy! All myths are one! Well, see, I think that's terrible. I really do. If that's all it is, if all myths tell the story of a hero who at a certain stage in his life blah blah blah blah, why read more than one? For that matter, why not just read Joe Campbell? [That's] exactly what he had in mind. Now his popularity does not depend on spirits. His popularity depends on his aura—legitimating the mysterious world of the East, legitimating the hunters and gatherers and their deep rapport with nature! "Oh, you like mushrooms? Mushrooms, too, let me tell you about mushrooms. . . ." Joe would affirm anything. He was terrific! It was a pleasure to be with him. Now with me he wouldn't give this crap about the great mother or something like that, but I would sometimes go after a session of some meeting we both went to just utterly depressed with what I heard. But ten minutes with Joe and a couple of bourbons, and my God, it was great.

Now, we could do that. And it's a gift. He had the gift of . . . oh, I don't know . . . societies that still honor the storyteller. We don't, but he had the gift of a storyteller. He had the gift. Unbelievable! And then the Irish drawl would come out the more he drank, which made the stuff more lilting. . . . But this is a business—and I don't think we show students enough of this—but this is a business that lives by high noons. It's shoot-'em-ups and rewards. Your job, in part, is to take somebody down. Their reputation shouldn't be a big deal, but obviously it is.

I say it when I gave those annual lectures for the social science core, that human science is fortunate, I have to say. We can't experiment on our subject matter. If I want to show what modernization does to a tribe, I'm really not allowed to sneak in a computer and hide in the bushes and just watch what happens. There are ethics committees that stop you from doing things like that. So you torture—there's a sentence in Foucault that says experimental science is the torture of the elements—to make it talk. Well with real people, you can't do that. The only way a person in the human sciences can experiment is with their mouth. We experiment by talking, by arguing, by trying something out—what if?—and see what happens. But we can't throw it in an acid bath. So the only thing that we have is to have someone come in backing us. That's it. That's not proof. But it strengthens a position or weakens a position. But it's really terribly important that if the human sciences are sciences at all, they have to have something analogous to [the sciences'] experiment. So talk is one of those. Comparing is another one. Experiment interferes with whatever it's looking at. It's not watching a natural process just going along naturally. It sticks a pin in or drops some irritant on it or does something to it or smashes it in a multibillion dollar hole. But comparing is doing something—bringing two things that have no reason in creation to be in the same pond together—throw them in and see what happens. It's the same thing you do when you interfere with largely, fortunately, an inorganic substance, but certainly we do try to cure diseases. We interfere with bodies, we interfere with bodily fluids, and we drop something in and see.

And that's all I do. I look at the Book of Mormon in relationship to the Koran. I'm dropping one in the other's pond to see what happens. So to me, if we're a science, we have to have something analogous to an experiment. Bernard really made a deep impression on me, his book on experimental biology, because he moved it to the living realm, away from the inorganic.[5] And he didn't worry—it was just animals he was working on, who cared? He didn't have an ethical bone in his body about all this stuff, did ghastly things with them. But he defined experiments as exactly this, the process of interfering. And that made an enormous impression on me because that's what I do think comparison does, among other things. There's no natural comparison. There's no reason to put something next to something else. You decide to do that, and in a certain sense change its context, because now that context is that other thing that you brought it to.

SUPRIYA SINHABABU: Have you had students that questioned their religious beliefs?

JONATHAN Z. SMITH: Yes. I think that comes with doing a course in religion, that people use it for that perfectly reasonable use. I'm sure political science has the same thing. Again, belief is a bigger category than religion, so I think that anyone who deals with what's mostly called beliefs, worldviews, point of view, I don't care what word we use. In part their class is intended to help them to settle. I mean they come with various expectations, and they will come and talk to you about them. You tread very softly. You try to get them—you certainly don't have an answer for them, so you try to get them to talk it out. What you try to urge them to do is to try to use some of the language we've begun to use in class. So at least there's a public language—and that's what language helps us do, it helps us bring our private world out into public without necessarily dragging every inch of our guts along the way. So if I can help them really think about their problems, but not underline the word "their," underline the word "problem," I think that's the best I can do. After that, it's friends, loved ones, ministers, et al., who move in. That's not where I go. But I do think that most people's problems with their beliefs, whether they're religious or not, it's not the first time this has come up, and there are people who have spent a lot of time thinking about that. So part of what you do is say, "Why you don't you look at thus-and-so, that might help you at least find a language to talk about this." It's bad enough that you're having problems; it's even worse that

---

5. Ed. Note: Claude Bernard (1813–1878) was one of the most notable French scientists of the nineteenth century. Smith refers to his book, *Introduction à l'étude de la médicine expérimentale* (1865).

you have to invent a whole new language to talk about it. I don't have to read your diary, and I won't. But where you are, others have been before, and some have made important contributions as a result of that. So that's the best you can do.

I would estimate that a thousand religions die each year. We're very limited in our sense of how many religions there are. And I'd say that a thousand come into being each year. A religion that survives its founder's death is doing well. But we still tend to have a much more limited view of the resources that are available to think about things. When people have problems, some people have general problems, but most have a particular problem. They want to say no, I want to say yes, that's usually what happens. Well, they've thought of all of that, so [I] say, "Go look!" The point of saying how many religions there are is to say that no religion, despite the way they sometimes talk, no religion's belief depends on a single thing. Because there hasn't been a religion that hasn't changed its belief structure multiple times if it's lasted more than that one year. And one of the things about religion is they take it all! They talk about everything! They're not like most who think they have a certain expertise so they pick their beliefs about this narrow range of things, and they're doing pretty good. You know, don't ask me what to do in the present market; I'm next to useless. For one contemplating retirement, that's an important question. You go out with the value of what it is the day you go out.

SUPRIYA SINHABABU: I was going to ask you that actually, are you retired?

JONATHAN Z. SMITH: No. I'm slowly edging. I'm in my 40th year here, and I'm 70 years of age, so it's getting to be time to at least think about how to make a graceful exit. Every time I've really gotten almost to the point of doing it I haven't been able to. So that's where we stand.

Anyway, most people having a problem actually have a problem. And yes, there are dramatic statements. Martin Luther says, "What think you of Jesus Christ is the only question!" Well that's the only question, but what hundreds of questions are wrapped up in that question? Religions will try to simplify themselves, strip off the things—they say, "Well, those are not so essential." But nobody needs to leave any religion over a single issue. Because fortunately, unlike some of our political groups, there are no single-issue religions. There really aren't. Part of the problem is they have no modesty. So they'll talk about everything, and have a belief about it, and it makes them fun. It also makes them asses sometimes. It does both. If your religion's been around a while, most of the members of that religious tradition haven't read all the literature of that tradition, that they get told is "this, which is it." The Golden Rule. The Gita. The Koran. They also, almost all of them, are a piece of a much longer work. In almost any field, if you're going to take a piece of something, you'd better take a look at the whole.

And that's where issues start. So it seems to me when someone has got the picture of the religion that it's sort of the *Reader's Digest* version, it's been condensed down. Campbell's stuff, it always shows you all the variety and condenses it down to the same thing. It's just too damn rich to do that to it. I mean, you ask me what I get out of it. I always tell him that to me, I get a feeling of the absolute wonder of the human imagination. It's unstoppable. It's funny, it's sort of a game among analytic philosophers when they discuss religion to invent something crazy and then talk about how you could invent it. And I always ask them, "Why are you working so hard to invent something? I could show you a hundred crazier things than you could come up with that are in somebody's most sacred writings." It's mind-boggling.

And the one who challenged me on it was someone who had a living rock. It could only go "woo!" or "uh." And how do you work out the grammar of "woo!" and "uh"? And I said, "You don't tell me how the woos got there. You don't tell me how these woos and uhs got there. I mean, you're a shitty mythmaker!" So I just picked up one yesterday—the world is a spider web, formed of the dripping, green semen of another spider that goes down the various parts of the web—I don't know what you call them, filaments—and congeals here and there. So now you want to talk about rationality—man, you deal with that. To hell with your woos and uhs. And that's only the first paragraph. The myth goes on for I think about 700 paragraphs actually. It's a Brazilian native myth. Wow! I look at that, I've never taught it, but I look at that . . . it's not that I want to understand it so much. I just want to say, "Hats off to you kids! You sold it to generations and generations! Woo! Terrific! Wonderful!" That's what I like about religion, it never fails to surprise me. Whenever you think you've seen it all, you find something like this that—"Whoops, back to the drawing board. My definition has not been broad enough. I have to get this one in too." It's good. It's good subject matter. It doesn't conclude, and that's good too.

I've always said it would be nice to drop dead in class except for the shock to my students. My wife's a piano teacher, and she actually took a student whose teacher before her literally keeled over in the middle of this kid's lesson. So I don't joke about dropping dead in the middle of class any longer. But I always try to—and I don't always succeed—to end the last class on an incomplete sentence. And that to me is important. Don't come to an ending. I don't think it's true, I think it's an artifact of the codex form, but the first page of the Babylonian Talmud starts on the back side of the second page, I guess it was the title page—the copyright page! Never underestimate the ingenuity of a man making a sermon. It's to teach us that we join the conversation in the middle, and the conversation 47 volumes later is still not finished. And I like that sense. I've always been sorry that political conservatives took up the phrase "the great conversation" to mean only the books they approve of. You have the great pieces and all the rest are petty conversations. I always thought that was sad, because I think that's what we really ought to do, and I'm not sure we still say this often enough, is that's what we charge you so much for. It's conversation. And you might buy it; your parents won't. That's too bad. It really is. They want efficiency, and I hate efficiency. Because it makes everything over too fast.

SUPRIYA SINHABABU: [Takes several seconds to riffle back to the questions in her notebook] Let me just dig back through for my questions here—

JONATHAN Z. SMITH: What do you want to know, how tall I am? Before I began to shrink and stoop?

SUPRIYA SINHABABU: [Laughs] I do really like your cane. I don't know if you if you've heard of this website—probably not, but it's called ratemyprofessors.com, and your reviews are glowing.

JONATHAN Z. SMITH: I've never heard of such a thing. And I don't like the idea.

SUPRIYA SINHABABU: Well, a lot of people on this website are big fans of your cane.

JONATHAN Z. SMITH: Well, I'll tell you about this thing, because it's botanical. This is a rhododendron. It grows from mama, it grows from under the ground, and gets out from underneath mama—this is a parable—and it comes out from underneath. So it's a natural cane. And what I didn't know, from the spindly, shitty rhododendrons that we have around here, that they grow to this length. I've seen photographs of them in England and they grow to be like trees. Feel it, it's very heavy! That's not my picture of a rhododendron.

My uncle—Freud is the only one who would understand this—my uncle had two hip operations and after they were both successful he turned to making canes as a hobby. I mean, to the rest of us—what is he trying to do? I have no idea. He made this one, in a wonderful phrase that I haven't heard used properly since the '60s—he was driving through the Smoky Mountains National Park, and he "liberated" it from there. I haven't heard that usage in—I don't know how the hell he knew. He used to be a YMCA coach. I don't know that they talk about liberating things much from a federal property. But he made three or four types of canes, and now I got one, from his wife who's 95 and said she didn't think she'll need a cane much longer, so she gave me the cane he'd given her. It was a little smaller and a little shorter. It's a two-handed job, this one, like so. [He demonstrates.] But the curve of it is funny to grab with one hand.

Well I think [ratemyprofessors.com] is an awful idea. And what good does it do? I mean, I've been married for nearly 50 years, I'm not on the market. What other reason would one have for such a thing? It's like reading a stud book.

No, I've been spared much by never—I've never seen the Internet. And my son endlessly explains to me that I should say that rather than "I've never seen the Web." I haven't seen that one either! He says I sound very ignorant if I say I've never seen the Web, but I sound like I know what I'm talking about—he has these tips for me as I grow older. He's nearby, so he comes by to check on the two of us. My daughter's in Oakland, so we fly out every now and then to check on her.

SUPRIYA SINHABABU: I was reading your essay on educational reform, "The Necessary Lie," and—

JONATHAN Z. SMITH: Oh, that one! Someone told me that's also floating around in cyberspace.

SUPRIYA SINHABABU: That's right.

JONATHAN Z. SMITH: I'm actually very angry about that. Those are notes! That's not the talk. And it was a series. And either right before or right after me was Wayne Booth, so I had to come up with something really smart-ass. He was the best iron the campus had, so how do you out-iron the iron? What this begets—and that's why not everything you do should be public—is a talk that's very situational. Certain talks, God knows I've given over and over again. But that one, that was a one-time only performance and deliberately done with one eye on Wayne the whole damn time.

I never knew it was there. I knew it was mimeographed and given to beginning graduate student teachers for one or two years. Then I thought it died an honorable death. And then somebody actually sent me a contract because he printed it as the appendix to a book he wrote. He needed my permission—even though he assured me that since it's out there, if I didn't get, it was the first time I heard the words "intellectual property lawyer," he was going to violate it with impunity whether I said yes or no. It's a book on religion; what the hell does ["A Necessary Lie"] have to do with religion? It's an introduction to religion, and I guess he wanted to say at the end, "Religions have necessary lying to them." But it's true. I think in there—I haven't looked at it in a long time—I also said some things about students and what they learn from us. And some of that is from real things, when I was younger and more ambitious, and also could carry more. I used to just take the students' books from them at some point in the class and take them home and analyze—spend hours looking at what they underlined. And there's a crack in there I think, we tell them, "It's all the process," and all they do is underline the conclusion or something. And I was shocked to see, yes, some did that.

There was one kid who took a black marker and obliterated everything he thought was unimportant. So in his Durkheim, there would be the word "totem," and nothing else on the whole damn page! And I say, not that I didn't know because I looked at the page, "What's here is details. Why do you think he put them in? He's not an anthropologist. He didn't go there. So why is he giving you all those details? So it's all about totems—well he said that on the cover page, you know it's about totems, so don't underline totems. God damn it, that's what the book's about." I'll tell you one thing, I said, "I wouldn't want you for my doctor. Because for all I know the disease I have you eliminated on that page! It's just details, get rid of it!" So that's the difference. What's the difference between you as an intern presenting a case history and Durkheim here presenting a case history? And the presumption is that everything is potentially relevant. It may not be! It may be misleading. But for God's sake!

So a lot of ["The Necessary Lie"] came out of teaching here. When I taught at Santa Barbara I had 800 [students]. When they left they wrote, "He had the hottest nightclub act in town." I was offended for years. By God, I would spend 10 hours getting ready for one 50-minute session and all they remember is that I tell jokes sometimes. Always with a point, they're parables! Sometimes. But all they could remember is they laughed. And the way some of them performed, I suppose that is all they remember. Those weren't the times for teachers because that was during the Vietnam War. And if you failed someone, you were going to kill them. It was a terrible time—certainly to be a student, but to be a teacher as well. It's the first time I evoked this principle of Marx because they had machine-scored exams. And I insisted on watching the machine do it. I said, "I can't grade it, but I'm going to watch it." And you know what? I found out it skipped 20 questions. So the students getting As did well—but the kids that got Bs were on their way to the selective service system! I mean this isn't just a matter of being pissed off because you got a lousy grade. This is sending you! You're on your way kid! And the damn machine skipped the same 20 questions all the way through the exam. And that's when I learned what happens when you can't see inside the machine. I finally started looking over here, and something wasn't right. "Some glitch," says the engineer chairman, "some glitch." That's why I trust no black box. Something that goes in here and comes out here, I don't trust. I do my Xeroxing one by one. Page down, peek underneath the thing, watch the little light go across, and then I take it out and compare it to make sure—and then I put the next page down. It's a black box otherwise, I don't like it.

SUPRIYA SINHABABU: The reason I brought up "The Necessary Lie" is because I was wondering what criticisms you have of the Core as it is today.

JONATHAN Z. SMITH: Well there's not enough of it, first of all. I understand why, and now I withdraw my understanding of why. I was told [curtailing the Core] was done to increase electivity, and I think electivity is a good idea. I also think being told what you should do is also a good idea, as long as there are options. But it turns out that's not actually how it's been used. It's been used to carve out spaces for double majors, to which I am unalterably opposed. One major is bad enough. I would like to abolish majors altogether. So two is unbelievable. And then you find out one is for mommy and daddy and one is for you, so then I thought let's take this issue head-on and stop this crap. It seems to me that majors ought to be flexible enough that if you were in history and then suddenly said my real interest is in biology, they might say, "Well, why don't you look into the history of biology"—I mean we've got a whole fucking library called the Crerar Library of the History of Science. I mean, they ought to be able to find some way to fit you in.

No, I think the Core, if it were a Core, is terrific. Now, the thing about a Core is it really has to represent a hard-won faculty consensus. I mean, it can't be "we'll put this one in for that group, and we'll put this one in for that group." It has to be that of all the books we could possibly inflict on you—only in ten weeks, and you waste the first week, you waste the last week, so you've got eight weeks. If they're not crazy, they're going to take two weeks to read a book. So you're down to four books. Now what that Core really ought to be doing is saying that if there were only these four books in the world—or the other way around, out of all the books in the world, these are the four books you should read. If they're not prepared to say that, they should shut up shop. That's my first comment. I find too much politics, too much accommodation. "We can't get the so-and-sos to join us unless we read this." And they don't care what it is, it's got to be a little bit of this, or the economists won't join the social science Core, or something.

That's the first issue. The second issue is I really think that if it's a Core, there shouldn't be so many of them. How can you say "we hold these truths to be self-evident, and by the way we've got eight sets of truths. You can choose which one you'd like to take." I'm not a fan of the fantasy of the Core in the days when on Wednesday, April 8, every student was reading exactly the same page of Plato. It's the automaton theory of uniformity. I mean, stick with one or two, but then it's five, six, seven, eight. The word fundamental means something or it doesn't mean something. And somehow, eight's too big. And I don't think they've made a hardcore argument. Half the time they got pissed off with this Core, so it went off on its own, like Protestantism, and went off to build a church of their own. And then you ask who they're speaking for. Now as soon as they've done that, after all the excitement of designing it, then they no longer want to teach it. Then they start screaming for graduate students or Harper something-or-others to come in and do it for them. So the other problem with the Core is there's not enough senior faculty. The more introductory you get, the more gray hair you have to have. Introducing is an old person's game; it's not a young person's game. A young person has just spent years becoming the world's expert on some itty-bitty little thing. And that's the last person in the world you suddenly give the overview. They've studied one little city or one little group, and now you tell them "all of social science." It makes no sense.

I once sat down at this long table in the Stanford faculty club. I was giving a lecture, and some people were supposed to meet me but

I didn't know who they were. So I sort of looked and waved, and they were very affable, they waved back! So I sat down. Turned out it was a group of physicists. So I thought, "I'll just eavesdrop until someone finds me." And they were having an argument about how whether so and so was old enough to teach Physics 101. Their phrase was "senior enough." I mean, that was their argument. So I think that's something we ought to be serious about. I don't think that "Lie" thing was a great piece of work; it was an informal presentation. But you've got to think through—you can't just think about a particular text. You've got to spend time introducing. I find that the more I know as a scholar, the more I need to use all of that when I introduce. Because out of all the things I know, I have to pick the things that I want you to know about. And I have to know damn well why it is that I picked this rather than that. I find that every skill I've picked up over the years is involved in making those decisions. It's better than a Nobel Prize, it's the most important thing we do. Because, just like religions, we don't study ourselves. We're transmitting. The great unstudied area of religion we don't study is education—how are they transmitted? It's not just mommy-to-baby; it's a whole apparatus they have. And how does that work? And is it similar or different? Religion and education—I mean, we're used to that as a lawsuit topic, but . . . most educational systems started off being run by religions. But prior to having a former system they had other systems. Anyway, that's digressing. But the transmitting is a big part of what any cultural system does. That's what makes it a cultural system. That's why so much public funds go to supporting it.

I mean, I used to be the Dean of the College, and I'd have to speak to the Board of Trustees. I just said two things to them: that we're the first country in the history of the world to have more teachers than farmers. That's an incredible statement. Now partly it's because these huge agri-businesses don't need many people, they just need to spread their shitty stuff all over things. So it's a little bit of a fake figure, but it was trying to make a point [about] that. The second one, however—education is America's biggest business. There's four percent of our product devoted to this. There's more people employed in it than any other industry. Why has this country chosen to put so much public and private wealth behind it? They must think it does something! So what do they think it does? Train you to turn a wrench—that's not what it does. Even schools that do that, they get asked to do civics, they have to make you a better citizen—all this other stuff. Well, I think that should probably be in the hand of folks who've thought about it. And I can think of nothing least likely than a third-year graduate student would have sat down and spent a lot of time—they may have read an article. Maybe they read an article by me because I spend an enormous amount of time just running around campus talking to graduate student groups who are about to teach. It worries me how many of them are about to teach, by the way.

So that's what I—those are things, small things. I have no philosophical disagreement with the Core. And I started off not entirely persuaded by it. I looked at Chicago's catalogue in high school, said, "My God, this is a fascist system." Now in those days there was no option. For two years, it was St. John's. For two years, you did what they goddamn well told you to do. And I wasn't ready for that. To me college meant free of being told what to do, so I wasn't moved to that. A Quaker college like Haverford never told you; it might try to reach a consensus with you and 24 hours later maybe you got there, but it never, never told you. So those are the kinds of things—and I think it's got to be a requirement. So I think it's a hurdle to jump over. "Now I got that finished with, now I go on to what I came here for." When, if we knew how to say it right, we'd say, "You schmuck, this is what you came here for! The other stuff you can learn, just pick up a book, sit down and read it!" Now I think part of it is we don't do it enough. When I helped design the Lang College in New York—it's part of the New School—a lot of Chicago people said it should be part of that school. So they knew about the Core and wanted to have one. What I said was something I used to do, again when I was younger, since I was the one [put] in charge by the president, to do the blueprint, I could say things like this, "I'm not going to recommend it unless they all repeat the Core their senior year." One quarter of it. Because that's when you know what you've learned.

I used to invite my class to dinner their senior year. I would pick one chapter of one of the things we read and said, "It's going to be like Plato's symposium, I'm going to assign dinner table conversation." I'd have enough wine and booze, Coca-Cola for those who won't, to keep the conversation moving, but we're going to sit around and talk about that book. It was not what we were going to do because as they sat down I reached under the table, in a careful style handed a Xerox copy, each one of the papers they had written. And whether they got an A or a D, they were outraged by what they had written. And I said, "That's what I want you to know." Our grading system—we don't give a lot of Ds and Fs—our grading system doesn't allow us to tell you how much you've grown. Chances are you got some Bs the first year; you're going to get some Bs the senior year. On the average that's the way it works. My God, what a difference between the B paper you wrote your last year and the B paper you wrote your first year. If you don't know that, you ought to get your money back. And by the way if it's not better, you ought to get your money back, too. [Former University of Chicago President] Hanna Gray heard I started making sentences like this when I was teaching—"you know if you say things like that it's not hyperbole. You're putting us on the line, shut up with all the you'll-get-your-money-back talk!"

But I really feel that schools—I hate these senior projects. They're absolute—every educational test of them we have says that they're an utter waste of time. They're a make-believe MA thesis or a make-believe doctoral thesis, and they're just a way of hiring graduate students to be lectors. They have more Latin names for them—rectors, lectors, preceptors—I never heard of so much Latin around this Protestant university! It's Baptist, we don't speak Latin! But this business of having a portfolio—that I believe in. Saving your papers and being required to talk about them your last year. Is it Wellesley? One fine girls' school—I don't even know if it still is, but a required project for a history student [was] to take a paper you wrote your sophomore or junior year and write an outline of how you would change it. Don't rewrite it—just tell us how you would do it differently. Because if you can't do that, what the hell have you learned? It's this production of . . . I've read a lot of them. They're not all that good. It's a lot of busy work, a lot of rummaging up notes and footnotes and that kind of stuff, and it's not clear to me that—I mean I would get rid of the dissertation, too, if you allowed it, but that's another topic. But I certainly don't want a fake one. I think all people have spent almost their entire year doing that. And it cannot be worth it. I think you ought to . . . visit where you were and see how far you've come. That's good for you, it's good for us. It's trouble for you; it's trouble for us. We have to find a way of thinking, we ought to find a way of handling that issue. If not getting your money back, we ought to do something about it. So that's—I mean that's what I don't like. It's that nothing's comparable to the Core [in] your senior year. And there should be. It could be one of these—this big ideas class, why can't you have a big ideas seminar for every single major? Constructed by its major, but all take the same topic . . . however many win the lottery or however the hell you get into that goddamn class. So senior seminars are good—what we're saying is that this is general education that will give you something to serve you well, whatever you specialize in—well, we ought to test the premise out. Let's test it. Let's say, "Well, now you've learned some special things, let's go back to that and see what difference it makes." And it should make a difference. Doesn't mean you say it's crap, but you should be able to read it differently because you've spent two or three years more focused. Well great, let's test it! Is it true?

So those are the things. I don't think they take it seriously enough, and so it's now become requirements, something you get over with your first two years. Or some hang on hoping that it'll be abolished, so you get the really pissed-off seniors because they're sure it's going to be abolished next year, but goddamn it they still have to take it! And all of that nonsense. So I would have added—they're shrinking, I would've added. I wouldn't ask college to fit so comfortably with graduate school. After all, despite our faculty fantasies, the vast majority of our students don't go on to Arts and Sciences graduate schools. We fudge it by saying we go on to—they go on to medical school, business school, law school. And somewhere in the neighborhood of eight to ten percent become clones of us. But we teach this entire College as if it's only purpose is producing clones of ourselves. And so that's why we're going to do the research skills in your senior year for graduate schools. Got news for you folks, that's not where they're going! They're voting with their feet, they don't want to be like you! They want to be like mommy and daddy, and they sure as hell don't want to be like you! They're going to go off and make money!

SUPRIYA SINHABABU: So when you were Dean, did you make [these kinds of] changes?

JONATHAN Z. SMITH: I made some changes, but not a lot. What I tried to do was to try to make talk about education something that was routinely part of the faculty's concern. . . . I thought we'd have discussions. So I'd form a presentation, bring up something from some educational newspaper, or something I heard at a conference, and try to talk about—try to suggest that college teaching is an intellectually interesting topic to think about. That it's not some extra, even some extra burden. They don't get as much work as they should. It's a no man's land. That means they get it in the major courses. And increasingly, which I despise, I see courses limited to majors only, which is absolutely horrendous. Some people have double majors, I don't know what this means, but anyway it's limited to majors only. It's too big otherwise. So then hire more faculty. Not going to happen.

I think, I once made the statement that I think if you're going to teach college students you need to know as much about late adolescent developmental cognition as you know about your own field. You have no right going in front of them and not knowing where they are. I mean I don't know whether the work of that terrific feminist at Harvard is still holding, where she says "show me a paper and I'll tell you what year it is." And it goes through—a first-year will buy anything from anyone with authority. A second-year won't buy anything from anybody, no matter how authoritative. Finally by the fourth year they learn what you call contextualization. Take some of it and leave some of it, they're able to take what they're reading, not just thinking they're going to push a black button or a red button. For the first two years it's button-pushing largely. And you ought to know that! It makes a difference to what your expectations are in a class! And also what you want to do in a class. If I've got a class I know has mostly second-year students, they're not going to take any shit from anybody, then I'm going to give them a lot of shit. And I'll argue about every goddamn thing they say, and I ought to know that! I wouldn't do that the first year. So, I just think that there's more meat on those bones than the faculty knows. And I think it's okay to talk about it, we don't always have to talk about the crap we talk about in faculty meetings. And again I think you can't ask, you're responsible to ask people who themselves are struggling for a degree to now not only show up, do the readings, maybe even think about the readings, before they walk in, but now know something about Carol what's-her-name's theory of—no, you know, and worry about how does the Harvard model of general education applies to the Chicago model applies to—no, that's not the world they are ready yet to live in.

So those are the things—I love the idea of the Core. When I was an adolescent and looked at it I thought it was absolutely insufferable. And I don't think I like St. John's. That eliminates the tension, which ought to be interesting. And this thing really is an hourglass—you start broad, you specialize, then you get broad. When you specialize you ought to be intelligently broad, not be even more narrow. And that's what I'd like to see the Core allow. I think it doesn't pull off—so it leaves this as a sort of "well everyone does it, let's learn a little about this and little about that, isn't that nice? And the next strand is to get some writing in there." That's overlooking the fact that writing for one subject matter is not the same as writing for other subject matter.

The other thing I got out of that book *Surely You're Joking, Mr. Feynman!*[6] that I quoted in that speech [i.e., "The Necessary Lie"] is that . . . , a guy wins a Nobel Prize in one science and gets laughed at for writing something in another science, not because of what he did, but because they thought it was important. At least in this book, I haven't read the rest. This is a guy I see in the bookstore. Of course there are tapes to sit and listen to Feynman in the same way there are now tapes of folks speaking beyond the grave, but you sit around and listen to the tapes! You get an aura. [Tries to eat a chocolate drop that came with his espresso without interrupting the flow of the conversation.] Oh I'll have another one . . . very discreetly.

SUPRIYA SINHABABU: No, go ahead!

JONATHAN Z. SMITH: My wife will come back and she'll say, "Your disposition's unusually sweet today!" It's an itty-bitty little thing! [He eats the chocolate drop.] Majors I think are of no use to anybody.

SUPRIYA SINHABABU: I really agree.

JONATHAN Z. SMITH: I mean it's . . . It's not real! It's all sort of simulated, and they keep telling you it doesn't get real until—I don't know what the hell happened, but when I was in my first year of graduate school I didn't feel a tingle. . . .

SUPRIYA SINHABABU: All right, well I feel like I've taken way too much of your time up.

JONATHAN Z. SMITH: Oh, you've just stopped me from smoking for a while, but if you've got one more thing to say, we've got to do it outside, 15 feet away. It's this new [Chicago law saying you can't smoke within 15 feet of a building's entrance]. Try standing on Michigan Avenue and try to find where you have to be to be 15 feet from a building entrance. You're on the dividing line in the middle of the street! You're going to get killed! And it's not going to be tobacco that did it, it's going to be some maniac driver! There's no place in an urban place you can be 15 feet from an entrance. I don't know what farm boy drew up this ordinance. . . .

---

6. Ed. Note: Richard Feynman, *Surely You're Joking, Mr. Feynman! Adventures of a Curious Character* (New York: W. W. Norton, 1985).

The American Scholars of Religion Video Project

INTERVIEW WITH JONATHAN Z. SMITH (1999)

The following interviews were conducted by Professor Alfred F. Benney of Fairfield University in Connecticut. As he described the video interviews (from which the following transcripts were made by Andie Alexander, while working at the University of Alabama): "the purpose of the American Scholars of Religion Video Project is to collect commentaries of significant American scholars of religion in order to highlight the process of their scholarship. The reason video is used is to allow the viewer to see that scholarship is the struggle to understand the question and simple print text can't do that." The interview took place November 21, 1999.

ALFRED BENNEY: What led you to become a scholar interested in religion?

JONATHAN Z. SMITH: I think the first thing that interested me in religion was when I was very young, and decided not to eat animals. And [I] was looking for some fancy reason for that, and that led me to read some religious folks who said things like that. I didn't know much about them, but it always was good when Aunt Tilly would say, "But you must eat chicken!" and I'd say, "The Buddha didn't." And so that was about it. And when I went to college I was a philosophy major, and I got interested in Greek philosophy and the theory that Greek philosophy and Greek myth were related very closely to each other. So I asked my favorite philosophy teacher where I should go to get a degree in Greek mythology, and he told me I should go to Yale Divinity School and study the New Testament because it was the biggest piece of Greek mythology around. And I, being very serious, did not understand he was joking, so I went to Yale Divinity School and studied the

New Testament; and that's how I came into the field of religion. And I've always thought that probably has been influential on me—it was not a lifelong interest. And part of what I do with religion and part of what interests me about it is that for someone who has extraordinary faith in reason and rationality it's so nuts. And if you can find some sense to the nuts, then that's a job worth doing. So that's what I do. But surely it was a joke, but the only embarrassing thing is that I didn't get the joke. . . . Well, of course, you know, in those days, before the change in the profession, because of state universities and all that, you couldn't go into an MA and PhD in religion out of college as a religion major; you had to go to Christian Divinity School and get a Bachelor of Divinity degree. Now, plus since I'm not Christian, that's a little complicated, and so we negotiated . . . to take two years of a BD. And I went and told my mother, "You know, I'm going to Divinity School," and her only sentence was that, If you come back a priest, that's okay, but if you come back a rabbi, never enter my house because I'm not telling you . . . , hearing you tell me I'm using the wrong pots and pans." That was the entirety of the discussion. So that—no, they always thought religion was an interesting topic, and why shouldn't one be interested in it?

ALFRED BENNEY: Are you a student of religion or a theologian?

JONATHAN Z. SMITH: Now I'm a little less excited about that discussion. I think it was a tactically important discussion when the study of religion moved into state universities, and we said a lot of stupid things about both the nature of the study of religion and the nature of theology in order to legitimate ourselves in an anticipated court action, which in fact, never occurred. There has never yet been a court case on religion in state universities at the Supreme Court level. It was a school issue that we've been relying on ever since. So I understand that distinction to be, essentially, a political and a tactical distinction that I think we've outgrown. I mean, I think . . . I've just suggested in a way what I think is the urgent question on which, I think, you'll find supporters on both sides of that alleged divide. If religion is a human activity, is it essentially linguistic? If it's essentially linguistic, does it fall into all the problems with a relationship of reality to language? Can we ever get behind the language to a reality? All these are very serious questions. Is there the possibility of immediate experience, or is all experience mediated, culturally conditioned? These are the questions that really draw blood in the business, and if you sort out the people on both sides of those questions, they will not break down into "theologians" and "students of religion." There are folks on both sides of that question. And I think those are the exciting questions. They also tell you, in part, who your conversation partners are. Who else in the university are you likely to talk *about* is more determined by which side you come down on those questions than it is that I want to put a label on me saying "student of religion" or "theologian." That was a PR set of differences, to be honest with you, I think. I have colleagues who would very strongly disagree with me, but I'm really quite sure that in the history of development of things in America and a hundred years earlier in the university systems of Europe these were ways in which you argued the legitimacy of a field; they were not arguments about essential intellectual matters. I think we have much tougher questions to argue about.

ALFRED BENNEY: How would you define religion?

JONATHAN Z. SMITH: Well, I would define it understanding that defining is not a terribly helpful process, but if I say that I think religion is a human activity, then I've got to find some ways of distinguishing it. I could make a lot of, I could list a lot of things, but they're all, in fact, as characteristic of the word "activity" as they are characteristic of "religion." So, sooner or later I'm going to come down to something like Mel Spiro's famous definition that it's a human activity that seems to wish to talk about and interact with superhuman beings, and does so through various culturally determined mechanisms.[1] I mean it's going to be something like that. That is, what tells me that I'm not playing sports, but I'm playing religion is that the players have suddenly changed their character. . . . So that really to me is not the interesting question. The actual interesting question is what I said before that—the interesting question is: "Do you think religion is a beginner of its own, or do you think religion is a subordinate category?" For me it's a subordinate category. People I have great respect for think it's a beginner so that you . . . There's religion and then there are kinds of religion. For me there are "institutions," or "activities," or "cultural

---

1. Ed. Note: See Melford E. Spiro, "Religion: Problems of Definition and Explanation," in Michael Banton, ed., *Anthropological Approaches to the Study of Religion* (London: Tavistock, 1966), 85–126.

formations"—you can use a lot of different languages—religion, if you want, is the genus, and underneath that there are species. So for me the urgent question is really not religion, it's human activity, and I think that's one of the big fights in the profession as to whether you subordinate religion to something else or you let religion be a stand-alone category.

ALFRED BENNEY: Is it possible to prove the existence of a supreme being?

JONATHAN Z. SMITH: Two or three different things: "supreme" is either an absolute term or a relative term. For most of the world, it's a relative term. For most people who think it's an absolute term, it is still a relative term. They mean there's a whole lot of supernatural beings, and one of them is bigger, tougher, stronger, more powerful than all the others. Sometimes they're honest enough to call all of those other beings gods, sometimes they cheat a little and call them angels, and messengers, and demons, and devils, and so on. There has never been, except in a philosopher's fantasy, a monotheistic religion. So if that's what supreme being means, then it's no wonder all we ever had for that kind of figure are philosophical proofs because they're the ones who made it up. That is, a singular supreme being is not a religious notion, it's a philosophical one. So you either . . . , your problem is, "how does one give rise to many?" That's a philosophical issue—that's really not a religious question. And so, the so-called proofs are almost all philosophically deductive proofs, and they're interesting. They don't help you much in understanding religion. One of the advantages of having so many figures is you can let complexity come up there as well as down here [points up and down]. You can have an argument among supreme beings; you can say one's nice, and one's not nice, and one we're not so sure of. You can introduce a whole lot of complexity. The more you tend to focus on one, you actually lose narrative power. And one of the ways religion does its business is with narrative power. Well, if you can't have conflict up there as well as down here, you've lost a whole dimension of narrative. So you have to find adversaries. You may have to demote them, you may have to kick them out, as some well-known traditions have done, but the point is that I can't imagine a more boring religion than one that was truly a monotheistic religion. By the way, as far as I could find out, interestingly enough, the word "monotheism" comes only into being in this late sixteenth early seventeenth century, and it's part of the Unitarians yelling at Trinitarian

Christians. I can find the word "polytheist" going way back; I can find statements that such-and-such a god is a *monos theos*—that's "one god," even though they had mentioned his wife, and his children, and so on in the same inscriptions, so clearly it doesn't mean "one" in our sense of the word. But the "-ism" word is an entirely inner-Christian argument where one group of Christians, in a sense, was accusing another group of Christians as being polytheist, so I don't know why we should take so limited and narrow a word and inflict it on the rest of human beings. It was a polemic, it was a polemic term, the Unitarians said, in effect, "You Catholics, with your polytheism (which is a terrible understanding of Trinitarianism) are embarrassing us before the monotheistic Muslims and Jews." I mean, interestingly enough, "monotheism" was a term used by Christians to describe other religions, not their own. And I think, a word that has that kind of funny freight to it—one ought to be awfully careful before one just throws it merrily, merrily around. All religions seem to show, at certain points of their thinking, impulses to try to pull some of this riotous complexity together, and at other points it gets too together, and they start to pull them apart. It's no different than what I said before, "somewhere between one and everything is where everything is interesting." So I think most religions are very good occupiers of the middle ground.

ALFRED BENNEY: How can a god exist when there is so much evil in the world?

JONATHAN Z. SMITH: Well, you see, that's one of the drawbacks of monotheism. Look what you then have to do: you have to then create an entire mythology. People, by the way, were supernatural beings in order to rescue your deity for what you'd done to him by giving him the impossible responsibility of being singular. Or you begin to go gnostic and imagine: my god! he's not singular then, or he's not the real one, or some other such thing. It's a terrible, it's a terrible problem. I don't know that evil is, in fact, as ubiquitous a concept as Christians think it is. In fact, I'm not clear it's an important category for anyone but Christians. And it's not evil, it's sin. Evil is already a wishy-washy translation of what Christians are up to, and if you use the more particular language of sin, then if you look at . . . , I mean every religion has a vicissitude it's struggling with—but a sin is not, I mean, Jewish material, it's purity and impurity. And impurity happens to be accidental. No one gets impure deliberately. So the biggest thing they can worry about is something that doesn't have volition attached to it. Well, then you don't have to have a very big mythology about getting impure. When a Buddhist talks about suffering it would be unfair to translate that into the language of evil and such sorts of things. So, I mean, one of the things that we have to do is be careful about the fact that, in the study of religion, we have exported a lot of terms as if they were somehow general terms. That's what I meant when I said earlier, "Yeah, religions are alike when they're translated into English." Because you've spoiled the native vocabulary, you spoiled distinctions that are very live for them, and treated words as synonymous that for them aren't, in fact, really quite synonymous. So every religion certainly has words for "I got myself in trouble." The trouble is differently characterized, and the "how I got myself" and "who got me there" [laughs] will run the gamut usually—because people are smart—usually appropriate to the problem. We also have to remember that most religions of the world don't know we have to be saved. Things are doing quite well, thank you. And so that notion that somehow, when you talk about "trouble" that's a real big deal—that's an illness for which religion may offer, in fact, the cure; religion may, in fact, say to you, "Yeah, that's the way things are." Or it may say even something stronger, "Your job is to make sure things continue to be the way they are." Our religion is not a religion that says that the way things are were turned around at some point, and our job is to keep turning it around. Lots of religions maintain this world. They don't know—they don't say it's wonderful—but they don't know that there's anything so essentially wrong to it that it has to be altered in any way. And I would say on a census-basis that's the majority of the religions of humankind. So then again, you have to be careful of an exception that you now are generalizing into a rule just because it's that exception that has given us the language by which we, quite naturally, talk about other folks' religions. If someone comes up and says, "Things didn't go well today," and we say, "Oh, it must mean he was living in sin or something" and we've gone ahead to already give it a huge translation, and all he might have meant was, you know, the world is just not, it's not perfect, but it's not so imperfect that I'm going to sit around and moan and groan about it all day. Most religions and rituals are designed to keep the world going exactly as it has gone. And every now and then we find a religious tradition that does rituals to say, "I'll make you born again" [or] "I'll do something else which will change the way the world is," but I don't really think that's as widespread as we think it is. Therefore, it remains the question, then, why did certain traditions get into that kind of language. And there I think you have to look at culture history, you have to look at what was going on at the time when somebody stood up and said, "You know, this is not the way it's supposed to be." And that's a very different question, and I think there are hypotheses; and good folks can disagree on the sort of historically causal element for why there is this apparent difference in the way you evaluate the world. And as you know, even within the tradition that likes to use that sort of language . . . , to talk to a Greek Orthodox in relationship to a Roman Catholic and one's perception of evil has . . . , is much lighter in the Orthodox tradition. On the other hand talk to a radical Protestant over against a Catholic, and they don't think Catholicism has any sense of evil at all. So that even within the family that is comfortable with the term, [it] depends who you're look at as to the degree of seriousness with which that problem is taken.

ALFRED BENNEY: Are there multiple deities?

JONATHAN Z. SMITH: I didn't know it either 'til a couple years ago. Someone asked me to do an article on it, and I thought I ought to start out with the word, but I couldn't find the word. [Laughs] You know, and that was to me astonishing. Christian literature up 'til the Middle Ages, or past the Middle Ages, through the fifteenth and sixteenth century, their argument was "true" and "false" not "one" and "many." It really is only the Unitarians that forced the argument to a numbers count rather than true and false, with the idea that one was true and many were false, but that was not the issue. If you read them, that's the major thing that they're joining combat on. Sometimes antiquity, too: "My god is older than your god." But not the issue of singularity—that's just not at the forefront. I mean, I'm sure somewhere is a text, but I haven't found it. But I've asked a lot of awfully smart people who know words, and that's the best I can . . . [sound cuts off]

ALFRED BENNEY: Do you think people would be religious if they were never going to die?

JONATHAN Z. SMITH: Well, the immediate answer would be if they're never going to die they wouldn't be human beings. And therefore, I don't know—[laughs]—I don't know how to answer that question. If behind it there is the notion that religion is a response to threat, to the unknown, or something, I have to say that I think that's a pretty uninteresting understanding of what religion does. Then, I think, we probably would have had a lot more similarity in religion because there are two or three classic ways you handle that one, and you could never explain why religion elaborates so much. One of the things that's interesting about religion—say, unlike science, which has a built-in modesty—there are things it will not bother to inquire on. It really will not want to know why you and I are having a conversation right now. Religion would love to be able to take that in—I mean, it has a drive to elaborate itself with respect to everything. And so I've always been suspicious of pointing to a *single* characteristic, a *single* set of questions, or a *single* religious figure, for that matter, as somehow generating the whole. It's one of the most complicated things human beings do—that's what makes it so interesting to fool with. And I just hate to see—I hate to think of it, is a better way of putting it—I hate to think of all that complexity coming out of something singular. But an easiest answer would be: it's very hard to know because finitude is after all what makes us who we are. And so the really interesting—and if I say that religion is a human activity, clearly, which talks about superhuman things, I would guess I would have to say that under that notion religion is a superhuman activity that talks about itself. And I don't even want to think, think out about the implications of that one.

ALFRED BENNEY: How has television influenced the study of religion?

JONATHAN Z. SMITH: Well, it's an endemic problem: on the one hand we know more. Television has shown people . . . , my daughter, by the time she was five years old, thanks to "Sesame Street," had seen more different cultures than I had seen in thirty years. So, on the one hand, all this diversity is there; on the other hand, what I think somehow one does in that is say, "Well then, you know, I have to use myself as a standard." I mean, there's nothing else to appeal to. "So whatever I am." I mean, you see it on the hot button cases—[former] Mayor Giuliani [of New York City] looks at a picture and says, "That offends me; therefore it is offensive." Well, that's not actually a very defendable case. But I think it's almost that we are too aware of difference now to do anything but say, "Well, then I'll have to trust my own instincts." Now what I think the process of education does is try to give you a middle ground on that one. To say, well there are some concepts that we can agree on, they aren't ultimate truths but they're not made up individualistically either, and we can try to negotiate between—"religion" is a good example—a category like religion, which scholars have made up, and what's going on out there. And at least it's not me any longer and it's not everything either. It's a middle ground—which is where life becomes interesting. Actually, just listen to yourself—life is awful. And if you just stand back and are just overwhelmed by the sheer variety of things, life is also pretty boring because if everything is different, then in an odd way, everything is actually the same because it's all different. And so the job is to find something in between which is "sort of like" but "sort of unlike" and how you play with those relationships are what I think makes things interesting, whether it's life or studying something.

ALFRED BENNEY: What do you think is the most significant question in religion?

JONATHAN Z. SMITH: Well, I guess the biggest question would be—and it's raised as a question—but the biggest question would be: why we, in our sort of cultural complex, have found it necessary, out of the complexity of human activities, to say we can find one in there that we want to call religion. It is a well-known conundrum. Nobody else has a word remotely like that. If you really want to falsify a translation, find the word religion in any other language. Now that's kind of a silly argument: if there's a word for it; it's not there—that's not a very good argument. But it is the fact that we have been preoccupied for a long time with finding in this seamless web of human activities the capacity to break one out and say, "When they're doing that one, they're doing religion." So I mean, in a way, to go back to something we talked about earlier, in a way we're the only ones who think there's a big deal about defining religion. And why do we think that? And that's an honest question on my part because I haven't the foggiest idea why we decided to do that. But it certainly is distinctive that we think out of a web of things we do as humans, the web of relations and obligations, and so on, that we have as humans, we can actually underline one set of them and say "That's the religion," we tend to do that: "that's the political," you know, "that's the legal sphere," basically a separation of powers almost. I don't know anybody else who thinks they need to do things like that. So that's a genuine puzzlement to me, and I have never seen an answer that is remotely convincing on that question.

ALFRED BENNEY: How do you respond to the idea that all religions are the same?

JONATHAN Z. SMITH: Well, there's a truth and an untruth to that. What people usually mean by saying "everything is the same" is, I think, errant nonsense. Since most of the religions of human kind are, among other things, framed in different languages, the best you would ever say is, "The way I've translated several religions into English, the words have turned out to look the same." It says nothing about the religions; it says something about the act of translation. And so to the degree, as far as I know, that religions are language systems. Those language systems remain as different from one another as language systems are. Now, if you go up to a very high order of magnitude, if you're a professional linguist, and "language" is now a category that you have made up to help your work, [then] there are ways in which all languages are, in fact, the same: they all have syntax, they all have certain grammatical features, they all have certain things they do with nouns, though they don't do them the same they still will notice them—in most languages, not in all. And so, if you look at religion as I do, as something that is not out there—people are not going out there, and if you ask them what they're doing when they're cutting the head off a chicken or jumping into water or eating a cracker or something, they'll never answer you, "I'm doing religion." So that religion as a category that we make up as scholars and say, no matter if you're cutting the head off a chicken or jumping in water, *we* know what you do not know: that you're doing religion. At *that* level, there is a lot of similarity between religion, but the similarity is the scholar who's created the category in the first place. I remember I had to give a talk once to a group of students at an ethnic fair, and they took me out for dinner. And I said, "Well, you know, I got a choice: I can tell two different stories; which one would you like to hear? That we're very different from one another . . ."—that's after a while, you know I think they were holding an ethnic fair—"[or that] we're all very different from another, but we're all the same under the skin; which story would you like?" They all voted for the "we're all the same under the skin," so we have this enormous desire to somehow celebrate difference and yet say that difference is, in some sense, superficial and misleading. But the only way you can do that is to ignore the world as it's given to you and invent some category that allows you to say that. There's no natural similarity among religions.

ALFRED BENNEY: What religious issue most interests you?

JONATHAN Z. SMITH: Well, I think the thing I've been interested in for thirty-odd years, though it's taken different forms, comes down to religion and its way of dealing with differences. I really started a lot by watching what I used to call the incongruity between what religion said was the case and what I also thought—because I don't think they're nuts—they knew full well *was* the case, and the two are disconnected. And, so rather than just saying that they were "crazy" or "pie in the sky" or any of those other kind of things, it seemed to me that they must know that they were saying the world was the way, in fact, it wasn't; and therefore, for me, since I presume they're at least as smart as I am, they would have to have thought about that—that would have to be something that comes out of the way in which they think. And so, for the first fifteen years or so, really, in my work, the words that would occur over and over again were the words like "gap," "incongruity," "difference," which gives rise to "thought," and that I think was my sort of note on the violin. More recently it's turned less to looking at religion, and I spend almost all of my time now looking at how people study religion. So my primary texts now are other scholars; they're no longer the productions of religious communities. And there I want to understand how scholars handle difference, and they handle it through a process usually called "comparison."[2] One of the worst things that's happened to that word is that we've allowed it to mean only showing the way things are the same. So when you write an exam question you have to say "compare and contrast." But compare is, in fact, always with respect to difference. And, so I've been spending a lot of time working on the questions of: "What is comparison? How do you do it? What makes a good comparison? What's it good for?" And in a period where we are getting increasingly nervous about comparison—I mean, we're great respecters of the local meanings and local traditions. Old-style comparisons are embarrassing to us today, and so to me, the question has been: "How we can responsibly, responsibly compare." But what's in common to both of them is that interest in difference, and I think most people, when they deal with religion, tend to emphasize similarity, unification, things coming together, congruence, and I've just gone the opposite direction.

ALFRED BENNEY: What do you enjoy about teaching religion?

JONATHAN Z. SMITH: First of all I love teaching college students. I prefer first and second year college students. I think it's the most exciting

---

2. Ed. Note: See p. 7, n. 2 above.

thing, as a teacher, to see an "Aha!" on somebody's face. For me the major difference between college teaching and graduate teaching is when one of my college students discovers something, I can celebrate it. It's an honest-to-god discovery. Now if you're a graduate student, you discover something everyone's known already. I have to tell you that, because I can't have you running out announcing that. And even worse, if you discovered something that everyone now knows is wrong, I really have to stop you from doing that, too. But for a college student, I don't; I'm not training you to be a student of religion. My failures go on to graduate school and become students of religion. I'm training you to do whatever the hell it is you want to do, and so I'm absolutely free to watch you and take great joy in watching you discover and finding out how you got to do that. Secondly, I think religion is a nice subject to teach because nearly everybody has an opinion about it. And in that sense, you don't have to do a lot of preparation to get somebody to have an opinion. The problem for the religion teacher is that they [the students] think those opinions should remain private, that religion is not really something you talk about. And so the problem is, which is I think one of the problems of college always, is to get a private perception into public discourse. And since they recognize that as a problem with religion, in ways they don't recognize it as a problem with a number of other things, at least you can frontally address the question, and I find that helpful. The third thing, I guess, is that it's a nice place also to begin to talk about what I think is what we teach as college professors: we teach people how to read, we teach people how to write, we teach people, above all, how to argue. And it's a wonderful place to begin to explore the notion that argument is not what goes on at the dinner table sometimes when mommy and daddy have had a bad day, that argument is something quite different. And this is a hot enough subject, though a private enough subject that the question of argument really gets at both of those sides of things. How you can come to speak about a subject and not hit somebody. And you know, it becomes a place to sort of talk about the processes of trying to be at least persuasive to someone else. . . . Well I also think one of the great mistakes that education has made is putting introduction as service courses to be inflicted on the young. Introduction is actually an old man's job. And I find that to decide what I'm going to do in ten weeks, knowing that most of the people will never again look at that subject is, in many ways, the most awesome responsibility I know of.

But everything I know as a researcher is into that judgment. It's not that you transfer what you know as a researcher to what you do in a course—that's a silly argument. But it's all the skills you have developed to decide if I got only ten weeks—I'm doing religion, the whole world, I'm not doing one particular . . . —what is it you're going to pick as an example? What would be an example that's so good that, if you teach it right, it could serve as an example for lots of other things. . . . I know of no larger intellectual task. And so for me, it's not only that I like being with the students, I like what it forces me to do. It forces me to work extraordinarily hard. I mean, it's the most difficult thing I know how to do, is actually designing the syllabus and the choices that have gone into that. And usually my first class is exactly about that: here are the choices I've made, here's why I've made them, and here's the price we're going to pay because I've made those choices. It reminds you, among other things, that it's not a natural topic. There's no natural thing called "religion"—it's the result of a whole lot of decisions we've made, and they ought to be self-conscious about that.

ALFRED BENNEY: Why should one go to college? What should one study?

JONATHAN Z. SMITH: At one level I think the reason for going to college is to get better at how to think, how to read, how to express yourself, and that's almost subject free, though some fields tend to put more emphasis on one or another of those characteristics than others. So at one level, I don't think there's any particular subject matter—if they're taught right, they're all roads to roughly the same sort of goal. Religion allows you, I think, to ask a lot of questions. It's a very diverse phenomenon. It's a phenomenon where, in certain ways, challenges are more surprising. That is, I think one of the interesting things is you deal with students—we've done this a little bit, but the one god, and evil, and so on—who really think they've got a kind of a picture of what it's all about, and suddenly the picture unravels. And now you've got a really very dramatic choice on your hands: you're either going to say all the others are false, but I think you're right—the kind of relativism, and sort of general liberalism, we have, "Well, you go your way and I'll go mine, we'll just agree not to discuss it ever." So it's not the false, it's the not discussing it ever, and since I think that discussion is how we do our research in colleges. There are other modes of research in other educational institutions, but how we do our research, our laboratory, are our mouths and we experiment with, with that. So if you'd want to say, "Well, you have yours and I have mine, and we'll never talk about it again," that's the place where at least, as a college teacher, I sit down and start eating. I mean, that's what I'm waiting for. And since I get you there, I can challenge assumptions you've not really even thought about—you haven't defended them, you just didn't know there were any other assumptions. And as a lot of that goes into college, then religion is a perfectly fine place to start off with—history is a good place to start off with that. There are some fields that lend themselves to that, at least, initial set of moves. Past that, I'm not sure I would make a case that religion is any better than any other set of subjects. I just usually get to where I want to get—as someone who teaches both civilization classes and social science core, and religion courses—I can get to where I want to get faster in the religion class than I can in the social sciences class, for example. That would have more to do with my limitations than the limitations of the subject matter.

ALFRED BENNEY: What do you hope to accomplish in teaching religion?

JONATHAN Z. SMITH: I don't think that I'm one who tends to make a list of subjects and say, "You're bereft, you're illiberally educated unless you've hit this subject." I tend to make a list of sort of—the fancy word's "outcomes," but I don't like that word—sort of capacities, and you've been illiberally educated unless you have those capacities. And what got you to exercise those capacities, I think in a sense, is uninteresting. I am on the other hand—I get too extreme with that. I once made a statement at the University of Chicago that I could teach a seminar on the telephone book. And I was taken up—a group of students said "We're willing to take the class if you're willing to teach it," and I said, "I'm willing to teach it if you're willing to read the damn thing, and you have to allow me, now, to use the Yellow Pages"—I mean, I cheated a little bit. And I did. I taught a—I did a semester long course on what we could learn about American culture if you were an anthropologist—who'd give their right arm for an archive like that from any other culture. What are there a lot of, what are there a little of, what things do we decide to put pictures with, what don't we put pictures with, what kinds of pictures do we put with them. I mean, why does every sanitation department put the same picture of a garbage truck next to what it does? It was a wonderful class. We had a grand time; we went on for hours. And so, I mean, the issue, to me, is—I mean, that's a little extreme—but the issue to me is not what you're doing it on. And one of the values is this value of your capacity to see complexity and not be overcome by it, but to deal responsibly with complexity, rather than either say, "Oh my god" or "I ain't going to look at it at all." And if you've done that—that to me is what ethics [is] . . . that's the ethical stance. If you're able to deal with that, then I think you're a responsible citizen, and I've earned my paycheck that year. . . .

But I hate the word "unique," obviously. No, I don't think I'm unique at all. I think that people do that. Now one of the issues always—I mean, you know, scholars, what do they do: they simply bring into articulation what are either—and therefore find interesting—what others just take to be common sense or what others just do without opening their big mouths about. And so, no, I think there's an awful lot of people who do this; whether they would want to say self-consciously that is what they're doing is, it seems to me, another question. And part of what scholars do is to make articulate what we think you think you're doing when you do it. You know, it's the old story that any foreign speaker of a language knows that language's grammar better than any native speaker of the language. We just know how we're supposed to say English sentences; we couldn't give you rules by which we put them together if we tried. Someone sitting over in Germany or Japan has painfully learned the rules—now the trouble is they don't know why we break them—but they have painfully learned the rules. And in a way, there's a necessary estrangement to know why certain things are happening, and what scholars are professional estrangers. They go to people and listen very carefully to what they're saying, but then they translate them, they generalize out of them, they articulate them—that's our job. I once had an argument with Abe Heschel: Abe Heschel's definition of a prophet was that he was a pain in the ass by the grace of god, and I said, "Would you accept a revision: he's a big-mouth by the grace of god. And if you want . . ."—and that's a professor. He's probably both, but in particular, he's a big-mouth by the grace of god. And what he's trying to do is to articulate what is held somewhat inarticulate by the subjects he studies. That's his job. It's not a big job, it's not an earth-shattering job, but I think it's a useful job.

ALFRED BENNEY: What is more important, questions or answers?

JONATHAN Z. SMITH: Questions always survive answers, first of all. There's nothing more dated, actually, than an answer. Because, if you're a scholar—unlike a layperson—if you're a scholar, you have to construct your answer in light of a web of alternative answers. And it means your answer is not entirely your answer; your answer is in relation to, with respect to, with opposition to, and you'll all go down together at some point. [Laughs] One part of that fabric is really going to be booted out that you still had to take seriously, and the minute that part goes, your answer is dated. You come up with a damn good question—those stick around. It's a . . . there are two things, I think actually. One is this issue of questions and answers, and questions are always better than answers. I certainly love the fact that one other nice thing for a researcher about teaching college students is they often don't know the cost of the question they ask you. It'll sometimes take me ten or fifteen years to honestly be able to answer the question I was asked. And they've forgotten their question a long time ago, but I haven't. That is, you would have no idea what it would take to answer a question like that. But in between the question and the answer, there's something that math teachers know and the rest of us ought to know more which is—that thing they always used to say: "Save your worksheets because it's not the answer, it's how you got there. And if you've used the right process and came up with the wrong answer, I'll give you partial credit." Well, I hate the notion of partial credit, but there are questions, there are answers, and the how you get from one to the other. And the ones that last are the questions and the how you got there. The answers themselves, as in a way that math teacher is saying, are more fungible, they're interchangeable. And there we differ in intellectual styles and different context in which this set of answers will look better for a while than that set of answers. But the questions don't go away, and the processes by which you get there, by and large, do not go away. And, so those are the stable elements in the business; the answers are far less, the far less interesting in the long-run part of it all.

Asdiwal: Revue genevoise d'anthropologie et d'histoire des religions

INTERVIEW WITH JONATHAN Z. SMITH (2010)[1]

The discussion took place in a Greek restaurant in Hyde Park, Chicago, in front of the abandoned church mentioned in the interview.

You don't have any email address?

Nope. We still have the dial phone in our house. My wife teaches piano and the young kids come and they want to call home. And they poke their fingers like this in the holes [of the rotary phone] in the dial and they cannot understand why nothing is happening. I find I never dialed a wrong number with that because my finger is there, and with those touchtone phones, I am always hitting the wrong place. My son tells me I am thoroughly analog. I have never liked the translation to digital. I like to know that what I have done is what made that happen, and not something that I don't know and never imagined translates it, and then it gets done. It bothers me.

You need to trust the machines and the technicians!

Exactly. I don't. I don't even trust my colleagues. Why the hell should I trust these things? I look up every goddamn one of their footnotes, so I don't trust "a black box."

---

1. Ed. Note: This interview was conducted on April 19, 2010, by Philippe Bornet, University of Lausanne. It was originally published in French in *Asdiwal: Revue genevoise d'histoire des religions* 6 (2011): 23–37.

Let us maybe begin with the beginning: how did you choose to study and teach "religion" or the "history of religions," and not another topic?

Well I did not, but I do not think it chose me either. I started off interested in botany, and I was going to go to agricultural school. Just so happened in that period, you could only study agriculture if you went to agricultural school. You could take no other courses, and I was interested in lots of other things. So I went to a very small College in Pennsylvania. It was a Quaker College and they did not recognize the category "religion" in the same way that they did not recognize the category "art." As a result, there were two things that were never taught there: art and religion. But what they called the philosophy department in fact consisted of people who did a lot of thinking about religion.

I was a philosophy major and I got interested in the old type of questions, such as what myth has to do with philosophy. I wrote one of my two senior theses on Hesiod, and I had read a couple of articles by Lévi-Strauss. I had punch cards in many myths and tried to break pieces down. While about to finish my studies there, I asked the philosophy professor: "Where can I go to do a PhD in Greek myth?"—"I do not think you can, and philosophy is right now in its most analytic phase, and even in the history of philosophy, they do not do it much anymore." And he added, as a joke—but I did not know that, I was a serious young student: "why don't you go to something like Yale Divinity School and study the New Testament. It is the biggest piece of Greek myth that is still around." So I went to Yale Divinity School, and I studied the New Testament as I had been told.

As a myth?

Well, that was all more complicated, but a guy named Childs had written an excellent book on myth and the Old Testament.[2] That was safer. One might look at what he thought it was, and transpose it to the New Testament. One could use that word and not get any trouble.

Now in those days—and it was the way this country was set up—before you did a Master or a PhD in a Department of religion, you had first to get a Bachelor of Divinity which makes you ordained as a Christian minister. But I am not Christian. I am only the second non-Christian to have done

---

2. Ed. Note: Brevard S. Childs, *Myth and Reality in the Old Testament* (London: SCM Press, 1960).

this at Yale. They looked up what they did for Sam Sandmel—the famous Jewish specialist of the New Testament. Everything that he did not have to do, I did not have to do either. So I never learned how to put water on the head and all those things. But I did take all the academic courses.

In the middle, in 1960–1963, the Supreme Court decision came down [on the unconstitutional character of any religious teaching in government-funded schools], and Yale instantly started a department of religion, which had nothing in common with the Bachelor in Divinity. It was located in the Graduate school, not in the Divinity School, and I was moved right over. I became their first candidate in history of religions. The great advantage that I had was that they had no faculty in the field. So I was able to entirely teach myself. Of course all over the university, there were other disciplines of interest such as anthropology. But basically I sat in the library and read, and it was a quiet wonderful way to doing it. I chose Frazer[3] and called him a laboratory of comparison. If I could figure out what he thought he was doing, this would be a beginning. So that was my topic, very early. Partly because I was in the New Testament, the topic of comparison was of considerable importance: that is the comparison of Hellenistic material to Jewish, and conversely. Both of them were badly done, but the problem interested me.

Finally, after I was already out teaching and just finishing the dissertation, they appointed a young guy who was a friend of mine as Yale's first appointment, Willard Oxtoby. He had to give me my exam, which I had not taken yet, because there was no faculty. He called me on Friday and I went on Monday, and sat for a week of exams. I then gave him my dissertation. He thought I had to empirically test Frazer, which was a crazy idea. But I finally thought of how to do that and it took me another three years. I thought I was done! Did Africans have sacred kings? And did they kill or not kill them? It was certainly possible to find that out. It was the only thing in there that I knew I could test, but I knew nothing about Africa. It took me about two years to figure out enough about who were those tribes, where they were, and to work the monographs and articles. I added a huge section in my dissertation, but I did not find it satisfactory, and that is why I never published it.

Since that Supreme Court decision, I always intended to teach in a public university, not in a private one. I thought that this handled some of

---

3. Ed. Note: James G. Frazer, *The Golden Bough: A Study in Magic and Religion* (New York: Macmillan, 1920).

these theological overtones. I also always wanted to teach college students and not graduate students. Thus, I started in Santa Barbara, which at that point did not have a graduate program: I was very happy. They then started the graduate program, so I left and came to the College here (not to the Divinity School, despite what they say). The College brought me, and I had a courtesy appointment in the Divinity School. I finally activated it, and did split my teaching for about eight or nine years. I left in 1977, and have been in the College ever since, teaching college students.

When I came, there was no program for college students in religion. The faculty held that the university was devoted to rational discourse; religion was irrational, therefore could not be taught to college students. So I went before the governing council, and said I had an urgent motion to introduce. They allowed me to speak even though I was not a member. I said: "I feel this so strongly that by this evening I want the department of psychiatry closed. That's all." Everybody laughed and they voted for the department of religion. Thinking that I was smart, they then made me a dean. For nine years I served as a dean in the College.

I have been interested and became a guy who would not swallow mosquito or eat a piece of meat at a very young age. I had found that there were lots of religions out there, and this is what had first interested me in religion. I had read the *Golden Bough* before I was in high school, the unabridged edition. I clearly had interest. But it was not what I thought I would spend my days doing. I still wonder about it to be honest. But here I am.

What thinkers would you identify as the main influences on your own work?

In true philosophy certainly Cassirer and the Neo-Kantian tradition were a very big influence. I wince, but I do not reject when some of my friends call me an idealist. That word does not bother me. I would not think that it is an accurate term, but I do not mind it. Cassirer was a very important influence on me. Frazer was only an influence on me in the sense that I admired, and still do, his ambition. Eliade had founded the College, and that was a very important influence on me. Initially for the approach, and nowadays more for the ambition, again, because I had problems with him, and I have written a lot about that. Durkheim is probably the most important intellectual influence on me, and through him Lévi-Strauss and the others in that tradition. And if I am an idealist, so were the two of them, or if they are not, me neither. But I recognize that you see everything through eyeglasses. You cannot get rid of those eyeglasses. They may be social, but there they are. That has always been rock bottom for me.

Those have been the people who have probably in many ways influenced me the most. There are particular people in particular areas who have been important to me, but as a general influence, I see myself vaguely within the Durkheimian area, though he never got clear about things like comparison. I just finished writing a piece in which I start off saying that Durkheim said something once that has been nagging me ever since, and I want him now to say it much more loudly: which is for someone in the human sciences, comparison is our form of experimentation. We are not allowed to experiment on human beings, fortunately. But if I am right, what we do with comparison is to take something out of its place, something else out of its place, and put them in a place that is in our head. That results in disturbing the environment of that thing, as the scientists do when they alter the environment in an experiment. They torture the elements so as to make them speak. Our way of doing it is by putting them by neighbors that they never intended to have, and to see what happens. In that sense, Durkheim on comparison very blatantly wants the word, and that is what he says he is doing, but he never tells you how he does it or what he really thinks about it.

How do you select the exempla that you focus on? I am thinking about cases as distinct as those dealt with in your articles on the Alaskan bear festival or the Jonestown massacre.[4]

Two very different ways. Most of them have been important in themselves and have been used to generate a theory. Most of the ones I pick come to me already italicized, like the bear festival: it was italicized by other people long before I got there. The question is then to reread the theories as well: I call it double archaeology. They have a setting within their own society, and they have a setting within our own society. If I have two things, then I got four settings to work with, and that is enough; I cannot work with much more than that. Most of those cases have been important that way.

Now sometimes, when I break out laughing while reading a text, that is where I want to focus. Because when something surprises me, it

---

4. Ed. Note: Respectively, Jonathan Z., Smith, "The Bare Facts of Rituals" and "The Devil in Mr. Jones," in *Imagining Religions*, 53–65 and 102–20.

also draws my attention. What surprised me about Jonestown was not Jonestown, but the fact that no one in the religion business wanted to touch it. Yes, it discusses possible understandings of Jonestown, but that is not the thrust of it. The thrust of it is about the attitudes of scholars of religion. The American Academy of Religion is meeting when it is going on, and none will talk about it, look at it, or discuss it. What is going on in the way we constructed our eyeglasses that this does not come through?

So it is either a 'pre-elaboration' or a reaction of surprise. In both cases, I contend that we cannot explain. Unless you do as those people working in the cognitive perspective, who, if they succeed, will be the first to genuinely have an explanation. In my world we do not explain, but we can translate, which is our way of explaining. After all, an explanation does nothing else than saying 'this is an example of that' and a translation makes it possible to talk about something in other terms. What they call 'explanation' I call 'comparison' and what they call 'interpretation' I call 'translation.' That is what it does. We do not use the same words, but it is the same process. I have never been comfortable with the 'science of religion' argument, because I think that we do not explain and we do not experiment. But I have these two things that are cognate: we compare and we translate. This is as close as I can come. Still, I get no thrill out of being called a scientist. A humanist is perfectly right by me.

Let us come now to the very category of 'religion.' What is your opinion on the idea that the category should be abandoned altogether, because of its colonial and theological legacy? I refer, for example, to the arguments of Daniel Dubuisson or Timothy Fitzgerald.[5]

The idea that anything is pristine, being a culture or a word, is absolutely nonsense. It is all dirty old bills that have been handed around over and over again. We do not have to take responsibility for everyone who has handled it. We do have to take responsibility, however, to be clear enough about what we say in order to block those peoples. You really do not have to take your own life to shoot those other people down. It does not get us anywhere. I think that a field of study that cannot name its subject matter is not a field of study. Look: Biologists study life. Do you know how long

---

5. Ed. Note: Daniel Dubuisson, *The Western Construction of Religion*, translated by William Sayers (Baltimore: Johns Hopkins University Press, 2003), and Timothy Fitzgerald, *The Ideology of Religious Studies* (New York: Oxford University Press, 2000).

it took them to make clear what they might mean by that word? So we should take the same amount of time.

The important thing that has happened, the revolution in my lifetime that cannot be taken away from us, is that 'religion' is a word, not a 'thing.' Those little brackets are essential, and it is a disaster that publishers nowadays tend to take them away from us. For at least one hundred years, a single quote has meant one of two things: (1) I am talking about a word, or (2) I am being ironic and I am distancing myself. I do not mind you reading me in either way when it comes to 'religion.'

But the notion that it is a word, and that words refer to other words, not to things, is absolutely critical to what happens to 'religion.' So when Gary Lease wrote that religion has no history, because there is no such thing as 'religion,'[6] he was absolutely correct: it is not a thing. Any dictionary that has a picture in it, get rid of it! It should only have words in it. It is not a bird guide. Secondly, he says: the history is to figure out, in a particular time and place, why such and such got to have that word applied to it; what makes it count as 'religion' here and maybe not count as 'religion' in another place at the same time, or in the same place at a different time. That is exactly correct. It is not always a political answer. It frequently is. But it is not always: it is also a legal question, etc. A lot of things are involved in that.

I would not get rid of the word. I would take all their arguments for saying that it is a case for being very careful about how we are using the word. But I do not think coming up with another big sloppy noun will solve anything. It is the problem of big sloppy nouns! The task is then to be precise and to actually take the time to define, to remember that a definition is not just a synonym or an example. We should really work on defining and the category will serve us as well as other words do.

In your article "Religion, Religions, Religious,"[7] you conclude by quoting an experience from your teaching: the strategy of students to refer to the list of definitions of religion at the end of James Leuba's A Psychological Study of Religion, *in order to show that it is a useless task. You add that*

---

6. Ed. Note: Gary Lease, "The History of 'Religious Consciousness' and the Diffusion of Culture: Strategies for Surviving Dissolution," *Historical Reflections/Réflexions historiques* 20, 472.

7. Ed. Note: Jonathan Z. Smith, "Religion, Religions, Religious," in *Critical Terms for Religious Studies*, edited by Mark C. Taylor (Chicago: University of Chicago Press, 1998: 281–82.

the moral of the story is that it is indeed possible to define religion in more than fifty ways, in a more or less successful way. How to know then what a successful definition is?

M. Spiro ["an institution consisting of culturally patterned interaction with culturally postulated super-human beings"][8] is successful with a slight modification. I learned from Tom Lawson and Robert McCauley to say, rather, 'superhuman actors' than 'superhuman beings,' because it gets ritual in there: actors are interactive. While 'super-human being' sounds a little 'belief-y,' 'actor' sounds a little bit active. This is a useful correction. Of course, this definition involves a theory, and I am not endorsing the theory. But you can make a very small modification to get rid of the theory. 'Culturally postulated actors' commit you to something. I do not mind this commitment. I am delighted with it, and so I will sign his definition. It is a working definition, but I have not found anything interesting that I want to call 'religion' that that one does not have.

I also like that Spiro recalled that religion is not the beginning. The beginning is the word 'institution.' Now we want to know, among all varying institutions, what is it that makes 'religion' a distinctive institution, distinct not from the universe but from other institutions. There is man-made built-in there, way before we got to religions, because we indeed tend to make institutions. I like this strategy: 'religion' is a genus of a wider category, 'family of institutions,' which is itself a subcategory of a man's field, like 'human creations' or 'human inventions.' In a diagram, we are at a level where we distinguish grass from palm trees, but recognize at the same time that they are both vegetables. It is not an ultimate definition. My god, ultimate definitions are not down here!

So Spiro's would be a perfectly good definition. I like it better than the one that focuses on the counterintuitive. Superhuman beings are pretty counterintuitive, but lots of other things are too. A scientist telling me about string theory is powerfully counterintuitive, but he is not being religious. I wish we had better words than 'superhuman,' but 'counterintuitive' is not it. Hans Penner says that if it leaves the house and does not

---

8. Ed. Note: Melford Spiro, "Religion: Problems of Definition and Explanation," in *Anthropological Approaches to the Study of Religion*, edited by M. Banton (Association of Social Anthropologists of the Commonwealth Monographs, 3; London: Routledge, 2004 [1966]), 96.

need a door, that is what superhuman means.⁹ I will stick with that. Luke tried that on Paul while he was in jail, he gets out and the door is still locked. That is the 'superhuman.'

I do not find it an exhaustive subject and I will not spend my life working on it, but I would not like to spend my life attacking it. There is a lot of wasted brain power out there, kicking around a very old chestnut. The minute you say: "look, the important thing about it is that it is a word, it is not a power, it is not a thing, it is just a word," the questions become: "why do we use it, when we use it," and "what are the other words that we use in relation to it?" And that, I suspect, is highly culturally variable, like all words are.

You said in another interview that studying 'dead religions' had a major advantage: nobody will come back and complain that you are wrong.¹⁰ But at the same time, it seems to me that the dead are more and more resuscitated for very present interests: I am thinking, for example, about the use of the Vedic tradition in contemporary Hindu nationalism. What is, in that matter, the position of the historian of religion?

That is not a new problem; it is not even a specifically colonial problem. People have done that to their neighbors for years and years. It is a human problem, and I do not know what makes it so sensitive. But it does. We redescribe people sometimes in strange ways, and that can bring tensions. On the other hand, the easy alternative that a native is the best informed does not provide any definitive solution, because what we have is everybody redescribing, reinterpreting, reusing. It is a choice between readings, not a choice between original and interpretation. There is no 'not interpretation,' no matter how far back you go. Everybody is mixed up. Everybody is from some other place. Whether an anthropologist says that he has found pristine religions or a Hindu Nationalist tells you that he has a pristine Hinduism on his head, it is nonsense. Both are offensive.

Obviously—what we have to do, and we have fortunately everything nowadays with DNA and language for supporting it—is to say that there is

---

9. Ed. Note: See Hans Penner, *Impasse and Resolution: A Critique of the Study of Religion* (New York: Peter Lang, 1989), 7.

10. Ed. Note: Interview for the *Maroon* journal of the University of Chicago, available online: http://www.chicagomaroon.com/2008/6/2/full-j-z-smith-interview (7/14/2010; this interview is included in this volume [see p. 3]).

no pure out there. No pure! And so there is no privilege to be interpreter or informant. Now there are some things that the informant could probably do better than the interpreter. That is, he can probably speak his own language better than the interpreter can. But precisely because the other guy is conscious—and we know this: 90% of our language in unconscious—he may actually see things you cannot see. That is what the whole issue of interpretation is predicated on, whether one is a psychiatrist or a student of religion. If I pay careful attention, with my eyeglasses and my ears, I will not hear it exactly the way you hear it, whether by the way we are from the same culture and religion or from different cultures and religion. Thus, the question becomes: whose frame are we using in order to make sense of those differences, for the purposes that we are interested in? Now the purposes we are interested in might in fact overlap, or be opposed. Both are possible. But we are not dealing with genuine and facsimile. We are dealing with facsimiles. I wrote once that the real issue for religion is not presence, but re-presentation. I mean that deadly seriously. On both of our sides.

We are in the task of criticism. We are judging the adequacy of those representations, whether they are native or foreign. There is no privilege on either side, as I see it. What they have mastered, when we study second hand, is the repeated representations that make a tradition traditional. So they have a little advantage: they can recite them by rote. I have an advantage since not knowing the rote I can interrupt you and say: "don't give me the next one, let's talk about that one a little more." That is an advantage that I have. Both advantages bring their own costs with them, and there is no costless interpretation. The ideal is to try to be as conscious as you can, to try like the Hippocratic oath to do no harm, or to minimize it, and to be as critical as you possibly can. At least as critical of yourself as you are of them: it seems to me that this is a mild moral obligation you go on. But sooner or later, you are going to have to add up the costs. I am not talking about benefits, I am just talking costs.

That is what we do, whether we choose between our theories and their theories: we are always dealing with costs. The sentence I said it best in was the ending of my article on Eliade in two parts:[11] that I would better go with my headache than with his [Eliade's]. We both have headaches.

---

11. Ed. Note: See Jonathan Z. Smith, "Acknowledgments: Morphology and History in Mircea Eliade's *Patterns in Comparative Religion* (1949–1999), Part 2: The Texture of the Work," *History of Religions* 39 (2000): 351.

But I have chosen that headache, and I rather have my problems than his problems.

You refer to the idea expressed by a student that Eliade was allegedly unable to explain Man, and you were unable to explain God?

Exactly. I am not sure I would sign this particular summary, but it has some vernacular truth to it.

How do you see the influence of political interests on the academic study of religion?

It is complicated and so very variable. You have an obligation as a professional in any field to function as an expert witness, whether it is to the public, to a newspaper, or if you get called before a committee. It is your job to try to say something to the world you are living in. The world is paying your salary. They have the right to get some return from it. I have no problem with it. However, I do object to a pre-canned agenda that tells me what are the points I am supposed to speak to, when I am not necessarily persuaded that those are the points that in fact will be in play at any particularly point in time. Of course, unless we take some funny monastic vow of silence, as soon as we are speaking in a classroom, we are always political. We are always trying to make some points, and we are trying to make some points about. Is this the sort of world I feel comfortable living in? There are various things that make me uneasy, and religion is one of them. How we treat the religions is one of them.

On a more institutional level, the political conditions certainly affect the academic study of religion. Thus, the moving to the public College in university created an economic space for the study of religion. It was a great thing. I do not think that in my lifetime I will see something equivalent to that shift. Three years before 1963: twenty-five programs in public institutions, all paid by denominations. You could have the Methodist religion department as long as the Methodist pay and not the state. Crazy! Three years after, 173 departments! I do think that if the base changes the superstructure changes. I have never seen anything wrong with that argument: It is fundamentally true. With that Supreme Court decision, the base changed. It is almost unimaginable the amount of change and this is still growing.

As you know, the secular round in America was a very religiously charged round. We are not like France constitutionally secular; we are constitutionally multi-religious. It is a very different starting point. The majority of people in this country, at least my students, have no idea of what a state religion might look like. They really do not understand it as a category, and that is interesting to me. Even though most state religions are in fact now pluralities, not longer majorities.

We have that funny history that comes out of England. We really bought the notion resulting from the action of a minority tradition member, which is a trade of being religious in the public sphere for being religious in the private sphere. That is the Toleration Act. We made that deal: we will not bother you in the public, and do not bother us in the private. One of the great problems this country has to face is that a lot of people who are the beneficiaries of that deal want now to call it out. A lot of people, a lot of religions never signed that deal. Islam never signed such a deal; it is unable to sign such a deal; it cannot trade the public sphere for the private sphere. The very left-wing Protestants, who are now right-wing, who were the topic of that deal, do not want it anymore. They want Christendom in America or something similar. We are getting the alleged beneficiaries of the deal asking to call it off. And the other folks, who do not see anything wrong with the deal, say that it is simply the way things are, and that we cannot call it off.

But I do not think that it is so much a European issue. Europe is more concerned with immigration and other sorts of issues. For example, Europe is obsessed with the question of sticking something on your head. We are largely in this country uninterested in that particular question. Immigration is here a boring topic since we are a nation of immigrants. Thus it does not play in the same way. I get every now editorials from German, French, etc. journals. Almost all of them deal with Muslims and ask why they are coming here. The answer is that it is like the Pakistani in Britain a long time ago. The British thought that the consequences of their failures would stay away and they never expected people to come back to live in Britain. They had seen the process as essentially one-way traffic. It was not in the picture, and they have been shocked ever since. Suddenly, the power of religion became an urgent requirement in the British school system.

On all those questions, we have obligations to speak and to try to find an audience. But I do not think that there is anything peculiar about religion in that sense. My economics department here, world-famous, has egg all over its face, because it did not speak out on some issues that it should well have spoken on. There is reluctance on our part, because the public world these days is so shouting and we do not shout well. In fact, we hate shouting. The problem with us is that it takes a long time to say things our way of saying them. So the crowd has moved on by the time we get to our conclusions. We are suspicious of the Martin Marty's of the world, of those people who come up with sound bites on any problem.

How do you see the contemporary situation of the academic study of religion in the USA and on a more global level, and how is it changing?

So sure it is changing. Its biggest change is that, to put it in one sentence, it moves from 'religions' to 'religion.' Slowly—I would not say it is a majority still—but it is the directionality of it. Indeed, and I am just old enough to be nervous about it, it is nowadays possible to get a PhD in the critical theory of religion without studying a particular religion. I always have been angry on the theory that you spent all that time learning a language, without learning any 'language of translation.' But now, just learning the language of translation without learning the language itself has its own drawbacks. We are beginning to see that showing up [are] people who are very good on the theory, but whose examples stink because of that. They run to the newspapers and say some little something or other, and by the time it is published no one remembers this little something or other.

That is however an irrevocable change right now. The kind of philological underpinnings of religious studies is weakening. The interest is not anymore a particular religious tradition as the authenticated mark. In the past, knowing a lot of languages and writing a monograph on some specialty guaranteed the ability to speak about almost anything created under the sun. Now people are trained to speak generally and the comparativist in me thinks that he likes it. Except that right now, it is a second-door language. They are not doing a lot of comparison. It is just 'bla-bla-bla.' It is comparing theories, and not the 'real stuff.' It is an overcorrection.

The second direction: America is for the first time far more conscious of its work in an international context, just as the IAHR [International Association for the History of Religions] had to get used to the fact that the international was not just Europe. I gave a talk last week on the next forty years. I made number one the Greg Alles global survey[12] of all the different

---

12. Ed. Note: Greg Alles, *Religious Studies: A Global View* (New York: Routledge, 2008).

folks from Europe to the South Sea Islands who have now associations for the study of religion. Most of that is done in English. It is going to make a lot of difference. We are no longer just dealing with people who happen to be from India, who happen to have their particular cultural constructions—essentially lay people without an adequate education in the study of religion. But we now have colleagues all over the place, and we have not paid a lot of attention to them yet. We will have to learn how to do that. There is no Esperanto, no culture-free language. That is going to be a big shift, and technology is certainly making it possible. It overcomes big economic issues. It connects travels, connects access to the libraries, etc. A lot of this is being overcome. Even despite my Luddite moments of wanting to do without technology, I recognize that the entire context of scholarship is in the process of changing and the study of religion is part of it.

A third change is the perspective represented by some folks who claim to genuinely have a 'science of religion,' I mean the cognitive folks, who seem much to be bigger in Scandinavia per capita than anywhere else, if I judge by what I read. It is like any field when it begins: it is a set of virtual thoughts. You cannot put them together; they are not harmonizable at this point. But this is not an issue. It is the way every field starts, with a couple of strong folks who lay out strong things. Then the second generation works on lowering the profiles so that they can be blended, and I have no doubt that it is going to be the case. It is not like taking LSD to show the chemical reasons of why we have mystical experiences. That was not a very good one. This one: I am too old for it. One of my rules is: do not read somebody unless you read the footnotes as well. And I cannot read their footnotes! But I certainly tell my students: you are young, get on it. This is going to be important, no matter what you do, like phenomenology used to be—whatever it was supposed to mean. It will similarly hang over everybody. Some will be good at it, knowledgeable. Others will do like they did in phenomenology: use a few words. But it is going to have that kind of effect. In that sense, it deserves attention.

What are the new challenges that the young students of religion have to cope with, in today's world?

Of course finding a job. We are turning out too many people. One graduate school turns out the number this country needs. The job is always a problem. Back in my day, there were fewer programs, so there were fewer students. That day is gone.

As intellectual challenges, there are substantive areas that, on the whole, the average historian of religion does not know what to do with. Whatever you mean by the word 'everyday religion' has largely been studied by sociologists and urban anthropologists. I do not think that it has affected our field very much. Interestingly, there are more Americanists studying American popular religion than people in the field of religion. Anthropology has been driven to urban areas because no one wants them elsewhere anymore. They have to do it at home. "We will not let you do it to us, but you can do it in cities." That is where the equivalent of natives live. Suddenly urban American anthropology is where the anthropologists are these days. That is perfectly right, and we should go with them. I once, at a history of religion exam, simply brought the Los Angeles telephone book with me and opened the section on churches. There were about 110 pages listed! I just invited this poor student, asking him: "Tell me about these, because they are right here. Just tell me about them." Of course he did not recognize ninety-nine percent of them. That is not a thing to be proud of. He probably knows more about funny groups in India than he does in this country. That is not good. The exotic turns out to be right next door.

The church that is abandoned over there, which sits right next to my house: I could have spent all my life studying that little church while it was still active. It used to have what they called the "gospel thunder contest." What group could make the most noise. I finally asked: "Is it because God is hard of hearing?" I was told: "No, not hard of hearing, but very far away!" But all right. Let us find out why they are beating drums at midnight. They are like the Dionysiacs Livy was complaining about because they blew the trumpets and beat the drums at night. The whole non-textual, non-verbal world is a large area that has not been theorized very much yet. We still see pictures dropped in texts as if they were mere illustrations. Gestures, rituals have been dealt with to some extent, but their treatment has been impoverished by not knowing what to do with the world of 'gesture.' Take for example the world of rehearsals: I yet wait for someone to tell me about the rehearsal of a ritual. We are still Protestants on that one, we are still iconoclasts. I am amused by the *New York Times*, in which each time that Ganesh weeps in India, it is an idol; and each time that Mary weeps in an Orthodox church, it is an icon. This is not an innocent distinction. It is how bad it is.

The material world, the visual world, non-textual, non-official, non-elite, non-self-conscious even at times: for all those non- we have to find positive languages, in the direction of what we are beginning to call visual, material religion. Of course the textual world is huge, and many texts are difficult to reach and master. This has kept us very busy for a long time, not realizing that there is like an oil slick on the top of the water, and we have no clue about what to do with it. That will also give us different conversation partners than we have had before, which will help us with theory. That has always been the case. We are largely a parasitic field with theory. We largely take up from someone else, and fix it up a little bit.

But I am not one of those who say that we should get rid of text and interpretation. That is how I earned my living and I continue. And if I was younger, I would still continue. But there is something blind about not paying attention to all that. There is something blind when we reduce a ritual to a text. If I tell you ritual is important, and I wink, I just told you a whole lot. You are not going to print "J. Z. Smith told ritual is important" because I winked! If you miss that, you miss a whole lot. We really do not know how to think about that. What we do is compensatory. I am tired of this focusing on text; let's turn to action. But often, even with a good will to do so, nothing happens, or a text theory is just changed a little bit and made into a ritual theory. All these left turns are there.

Maybe the internationalization of the study of religion will help.

Exactly. Our taking for granted is not theirs and vice versa.

What current projects are you working on?

I am still trying to do a project on encounters, dealing with Columbus. I have got cartons and cartons of documentation. But I stopped because of the last book, and because new Columbian documents were found before I could finish it. We will see if I can absorb all the new data. I may chisel some short pieces out. I had planned this project in order to deal with the other kind of difference, by following that particular way in a perspective of encounters.

There is also a project dealing with those myths that are all over the place, which explain why we are all of different colors. One goal is here to look at when it became a really urgent question at different places at different times, and to work with native theories of that outcome. There are hundreds of these stories out there. At the end of his life Eliade told something important, one of the rare things that he ever said that sticks with me still. He had spent his whole life on cosmic myths and the more he was advancing in his old age—in his 70s or something—the more he realized he never focused on the ancestral myths of transformation, and called that a second kind of beginning. I always thought that it is actually the most interesting one. The cosmos is big, but this kind of story is taking us back home. Since he did not do it, I thought that I could work on this same material, but from another perspective. I might finish it, or not: I am not as well physically than in the past. Next year [2010–2011], I could discontinue my teaching. If this is the case, it would be over, since I never published anything that has not been generated and tested in a classroom.

The Devil in Mr. Smith

A CONVERSATION WITH JONATHAN Z. SMITH (2012)

Jonathan Z. Smith, University of Chicago (Emeritus)
Thomas Pearson, Wabash Center
Eugene V. Gallagher, Connecticut College
Tim Jensen, University of Southern Denmark
Satoko Fujiwara, University of Tokyo

This interview was recorded in November 2012 in Jonathan Z. Smith's Hyde Park graystone. Professor Smith offers insights into how he thinks about his classroom teaching and his students' learning through descriptions of various assignments and classroom activities he has developed over more than forty years of teaching. The discussion ranges broadly over such topics as: how students read, the failure to adequately prepare graduate students as teachers, students' faith commitments, the use of newspapers (and humor) in the classroom, and the role of definition, de-familiarization, and critique of the study of religion in introductory classes. The discussion presents vivid glimpses into Jonathan Z. Smith's teaching practice and his teaching persona, including the time a student brought a minister to class to do an exorcism because she thought Smith was the Devil.

THOMAS PEARSON: Thank you for having us today for this conversation. Your essays on the history and methods of the study of religion have been widely influential in the field for a generation. And what's truly remarkable for a scholar of your achievement and influence on the guild is that you have also written quite extensively and substantively about our shared profession as teachers. Your well-known essays that interrogate the research assumptions and preoccupations of the discipline are matched by your insightful interrogations of the assumptions underlying teaching. You have been especially articulate about the role of introductory religion courses in the humanities curriculum.

But we thought today we would encourage you to explore not the curriculum and content of religion courses but the pedagogies of classroom teaching practices. So let me start with this area of questioning: Is there anything like a distinctive pedagogy for teaching religious studies? Should there be? How would you describe your teaching practices? How would you characterize the teaching practices of your colleagues in the field?

JONATHAN Z. SMITH: Well, I don't think I want to concede that there's a particular pedagogy for religious studies. I think basically I've always thought we teach reading and writing, acknowledging that this instruction is not entirely discipline free. At the undergraduate level we ought not be thinking that we are training professionals in the field.

There are, however, certain problems that present themselves in the religious materials we study in class, which don't often have analogies in materials used in other disciplines. You alluded to one of them in our earlier correspondence: students' experiential or faith commitment to the material is probably louder in religious studies than in other fields. It's not entirely absent in other fields but it is something that needs to be attended to in our field especially. If you're not conscious of it you might be surprised when it disrupts the class.

But, no, I don't think there are pedagogies peculiar to the field of religion. I suspect our teaching is rather in the spectrum of things that liberal arts teachers do. We're probably more wedded to the text than some other fields are. We certainly don't really have a very effective idea of what a hands-on lab component of a class would be. We ask students to write essays, which is not really the same thing as a lab. I probably put more emphasis on how you read than a physics instructor would. So I think there are differences, but I don't think they are telling. Certainly I don't think a religion professor could simply wander into another discipline's classroom, but then I don't think you could wander into another professor's classroom within our own field either.

I remember during my first year at Santa Barbara I was given a semester off from teaching to finish my dissertation, and the instructor they hired to teach my class thought he could just use the syllabus that

I had developed. He called me almost immediately, asking: "Why is this assignment next to this other assignment? Why are you talking about this person? What kind of nonsense is this?" et cetera, et cetera. No one can teach another's syllabus. That's why I rarely publish my syllabi. I get so many requests to provide a syllabus for various publication projects and so on, but I think they're useless. Someone else's syllabus can suggest a reading you might not have thought of, so it might have a certain primitive value. But what we do in our courses is probably more personally idiosyncratic than disciplinarily idiosyncratic. I think there are more differences between individual instructors than there are differences between different fields such as English literature and religion.

THOMAS PEARSON: So how would you describe your own idiosyncratic method in the classroom?

JONATHAN Z. SMITH: I have a whole host of things that I do, and I try to do many different things—sometimes reinforcing something I've done in a previous class session, sometimes doing something different, purposively. I play a different role each time. In many of my classes I require short reading reports each week. This is helpful because by the time we get to the large final essay I have already interacted with a student's writing ten times or more. (And I think it's important to read and return these short reading reports by the next class session, or the students don't remember what they've written, they've moved on.) Reading is the key to what they're doing in the course—and it is the one thing I can't watch them do (without violating all kinds of privacy laws). These reading reports give me some sense of how they're reading and I can react if there's something that troubles me. I always take the first ten minutes or so in class to discuss what I learned from their reading reports.

This is the place where I often handle the issues involving their faith commitments if they arise. I usually have one reading report assignment early on designed precisely to smoke this issue out. Because this issue probably looms larger for us than it does in other fields (although I suspect it may play a role in political science and if philosophers would teach something other than linguistic analysis we would probably get it there too).

Another thing I found very helpful is to collect their books to see how they have been underlining or making notes in the margins. Their schmearing on the page really tells me what they're looking for in the reading, what they think is important. In contrast, they usually tip their questions in class to what they think I'm looking for; but they don't tip that yellow schmear on the page of their book. So I have found that, although it takes a lot of time, it is enormously useful to actually collect their books and inspect the pages for their notes and schmears.

I have found funny cases. I may have mentioned this in something I wrote, but there was one kid who obliterated with black ink everything that he thought wasn't important. It was like the old communist-style censorship. And in another case, a student explained to me that she was interested only in Durkheim's facts; she had highlighted every little stupid detail about the Aborigines putting the feathers on the right buttock and then moving it to the left buttock, et cetera, et cetera—but she had no use for any of his "opinions" about society, just the facts. That's a gift from God to spot something like that. The whole class benefited from that, because if one student had that notion then others did too.

TIM JENSEN: I'd like to ask you about what I call "*Forschungsgeschichte*"—or the study of the history of the study of (the history) of religion. That is a very demanding field. In Denmark where I teach, I am preparing students to teach in the secondary school system. I have them for a three-year course of study. I am able to introduce the basics of the study of religion in the introductory course and then move on in subsequent courses to these more difficult issues. But you have written about the norm in the United States in which most of your students take only a single introductory course and never another one after that. So how do you broach the more complicated issues in the study of the history of the study of religion?

JONATHAN Z. SMITH: It means the pressure is enormous because for most students that one course is it. You can't have in mind in an intro course that you're laying the pathway to a PhD. I don't try to introduce them to the study of the study. But I do introduce them to the history of the words.

Students don't generally understand the weight that words are carrying. So we pause over words so that I might impress on them the importance of using a historical dictionary. I try to show them, for example, that the meanings of the terms "objective" and "subjective" reversed from the eighteenth to the nineteenth century; each took on the meaning that the other one had. That's handy to know if you're going to be reading those historical texts. But it tells them something more than that. It teaches them that our major tool in the humanities is words. It is important for students to realize that we are stuck with the terminology we inherit. I try to get at this in part by staging the readings. In the first three weeks of the course the readings keep hitting on the problems of definition, on our relationship to the material—but without being all that explicit about it.

I lay little booby traps for them. The first thing we read that isn't about definitions of religion and such [is] a selection from Schärer's *Ngaju Religion*.[1] We read the cosmogonic myth in there. Outside of the fact that it's a fairly extraordinary myth my reason for reading it is that I know that they're going to bite on the phrase "Tree of Life" in the myth. They're going to get all excited over it. Some of them will think, "Thank God. This proves that Christianity is universal. You see, even these naked savages know about the tree of life." I get reading reports on this. And that gives me the opportunity to address this in class. The reason why I picked this text is that he [Schärer] is a missionary. So that allows the question about words to come up in another sort of way. I tell them that this may be an overly Christian translation, but that I see nothing wrong with the phrase "Tree of Life." I see it used in a wide variety of cultures that do not share influences. But what's the difference in how the words are used? Well, to make a long story short, one of the big differences is that in this myth two deities have a fight and by accident knock some moss and bark off the tree and out of that comes the first man and first woman. I can show them that an accidental creation is far from the "Tree of Life" in the Genesis story. It's nice that they saw something familiar in the text. You have to recognize that instinct. They're desperate for something familiar if you're not just teaching them their own tradition. So I tell them it's good that they found something familiar. This is what a philologist would call a false friend—they abound in this business. You just have to be alert to it. In this particular case the differences become more important than what is probably just an accidental verbal similarity.

The point is, I try to select the readings not only for their content and for advancing the overall narrative of the class, but also because

---

1. Ed. Note: Hans Schärer, *Ngayu Religion: The Conception of God among a South Borneo People*, translated by R. Needham (The Hague: Martinus Nijhoff, 1963).

I think certain ones will provoke some fairly predictable responses that will be useful. And because I'm getting a reading report from them every week I can keep track of responses and I can intervene. I don't have to wait until the last paper. By then there's nothing to intervene in because they're gone. For most of them that will be the first and only paper they will ever in their lives write on religion. It's not a grand finale. Interventions have to be done before that paper. The final paper allows you to see whether with a different sort of assignment they remember to address the sorts of things you've been showing them through the semester.

I don't give them free papers. They're told what to write a final paper on. They are to take their initial definitions of religion that I asked them to write in the first five minutes of class and revise them with specific reference to materials we've read and to our class discussions. This assignment shows them the ethic of revision and being self-reflective. On the whole I've been very pleased with this assignment. I haven't changed it for ten years. They all know it's coming; they're told in the syllabus. There's no reason why they shouldn't be thinking about the final exercise as they go through the course.

But to return to your question, I think that at the undergraduate level it is over-professionalization to focus on theory. I think it is more properly part of graduate training, which, if it is any good, ought to force you to understand and critique the theory but also in some way to employ it. But this is a distraction from what I want to be doing with my average "Introduction to Religion" course. The students don't come to the class with the questions those theories are designed to deal with. Their questions are: Is it true? And how can someone believe something like this? Their questions are highly value-laden.

EUGENE GALLAGHER: Have you given any thought to the fact that students taking the introductory religion course have had no high school preparation, in contrast to other undergraduate disciplines such as English or chemistry, which have been part of the secondary school curriculum?

JONATHAN Z. SMITH: If they've had any study of religion it has been in religious school, which is not helpful. For the majority of our students this will be the first and only religion course they'll ever take, and that means that you shouldn't teach as though you're recruiting majors and future scholars in the field, or you'll miss what's most important for your students.

TIM JENSEN: It is interesting, again, to compare this with the context where I teach in Denmark. I said earlier that our curriculum is oriented toward preparing our students to be teachers of religion in the primary and secondary school system. Thus in Denmark we have a fairly good religion education program and I can count on students coming into my university classroom having a more or less solid knowledge base. This is how we have survived as a discipline in the university system, by preparing our students to become teachers of religion education in primary and secondary schools, and then receiving their graduates in our university classrooms with an already somewhat developed knowledge of the field.

JONATHAN Z. SMITH: No, we don't have that at all in the United States. And it's interesting to see that almost every professional society has an education journal because they're involved in preparing teachers for their disciplines beginning at the primary school level. History has a deep interest in what's going on in primary school education, as do English and math and the sciences. In religion we are sealed off from all of that and so teaching becomes more of an avocation than a vocation in our field. It might be a hobby but it's not part of your dossier. That makes religion somewhat peculiar in the university curriculum: we have no colleagues in primary and secondary education. This explains to me why the link between religion and education—which has from the beginning always been a very strong link—is rarely studied as a dissertation topic. We have very few studies that look at the educational function of religion. We're beginning to get more studies on law, which is also very important in religion, but education still is not on our map. And I think this is because religion education in the United States is confined to a very small portion of the life cycle of the student (except in parochial schools, of course). So it's not an obvious topic. Even highly esoteric fields, after all, have a curriculum for general physics or general chemistry in high school, if not earlier. So we have this funny situation where you can't take a basic knowledge of religion for granted when students walk into your classroom and you have to stage activities to find out what they do know—and also what they may be concealing.

TIM JENSEN: You wrote in an essay titled "Basic Problems in the Study of Religion" that "the role of a college teacher is to be precisely that of insuring that his students have 'wrinkles on their brows' and that they become adept in the 'hermeneutics of suspicion.'"[2]

JONATHAN Z. SMITH: Yes. But I would add that my aim is that they not be defeated by that. I want it to be a spur to more thought, not a blockage or impediment. "Wrinkles on the brow" is the most basic definition I have of the teaching enterprise. We enable wrinkles. And then there's the "suspicion" part. My goal is that they not fall for it: "Don't be taken in by it; use the skills of critical inquiry that we've been teaching you, allegedly." I think there are some students who are genuinely frustrated. They want the last day to be some sort of summing up. But for me, the last day is always a day of questions. I require students to submit them in writing in advance. I want to know what really pissed them off. What's the biggest problem they've had? I try to tell them that I recognize their problem and that it's a real problem. It's not that I've withheld an answer from them. Hopefully it's a much better problem than they raised on the first day of class. And I want them to see that it's okay that there is this problem. It really is.

THOMAS PEARSON: Do you think learning happens when students feel disturbed? Is that an important moment?

JONATHAN Z. SMITH: It's a moment, certainly. But you can't keep it. You can't disturb students for fifty minutes without end because they won't be back the next day.

THOMAS PEARSON: There's the important element of resistance, where they refuse to learn.

JONATHAN Z. SMITH: That's right. Or they just say, there he goes again (which is actually the worst). It can be devastating once they think you've gotten on your hobby horse again. So you have to be very careful. You can use humor, but you can't be flip. Sarcasm doesn't work, although I'm very tempted sometimes.

THOMAS PEARSON: It's misinterpreted?

---

2. Ed. Note: Jonathan Z. Smith, "Basic Problems in the Study of Religion," in *On Teaching Religion: Essays by Jonathan Z. Smith*, edited by Christopher Lehrich (New York: Oxford University Press, 2013), 27.

JONATHAN Z. SMITH: They write things down and they don't know I was kidding. So you don't want to be sarcastic. But, on the other hand you're trying to model that you don't have to get all serious and speak in Latin just because you're talking religion. You don't have to wear a black suit and look solemn. It's a perfectly fun field of study. You want to let that happen. But you want to draw the difference between having fun and "making fun of." Sometimes I go to extraordinary lengths to show why something that appears patently ridiculous may not be so ridiculous after all. On the other hand, it seems to me at times, that you just have to say, "I really—try as I will—can't understand this one." That usually comes up when someone asks me something. It's not built into the course.

THOMAS PEARSON: Returning to something you said earlier about students' discovery of the tree of life in the cosmogonic myth, it seems to me that in part why learning can take place there is that it starts with recognition. You take what's exotic and make it familiar.

JONATHAN Z. SMITH: That's right. But then you have to do the opposite too. But I start by saying, "Good, you found a point you can relate to in this complicated, crazy story where mountains are talking to each other and so on. That's important. Now however, you have to think about the text that you found a way into and you have to ask yourself if that story really is talking about what you think you're relating to it? Is this really the way the actors in this particular narrative are acting?" And the answer, I think, is probably no. And then also you have to take the familiar and make it exotic. I use the Bible a lot in class, and when I get through, it's not the Bible they've ever seen.

THOMAS PEARSON: So you take the exotic and make it familiar, and take the familiar and make it exotic.

JONATHAN Z. SMITH: Yes. They hear this from the very first day: familiarization and de-familiarization. These are two of the very few technical sounding terms that I hit them with right away, and keep hitting them with—because it's both. The whole art of the business is how you balance those two apparently contrary impulses. What's useful is that it's not just a question of the difference between us and them. It can also be the difference between us and our own past. That's why the Bible plays such an important role in my class. I ask them: "Did it always mean what you just told me it means?"

SATOKO FUJIWARA: In this context, your famous line in the introduction to *Imagining Religion* that there is no data for religion has, I think, played a very de-familiarizing role. How do students respond to that?

THOMAS PEARSON: That's de-familiarizing for the academic professionals, as opposed to our students, isn't it. It de-familiarizes us from what we thought we were doing.

JONATHAN Z. SMITH: If I had a nickel for every time that sentence has been quoted I could have retired forty years ago. But I have to say that sometimes the way the quote is used is de-familiar to me! I wasn't saying we should abolish the term, for example. I didn't think I was saying anything very significant when I wrote that. I thought it was a self-evident proposition and I just went on.

I don't know that I have ever taught that text to undergraduates. Instead, I come at it in the context of the definitions I ask them to write on the first day of class. Right at the beginning of the course I ask them to write a little essay telling me what religion is and what the study of religion is. I take a cigarette break outside and when I come back it has to be done. I collect their definitions. And then I say what we have to do is define definition. I say there are a lot of general nouns like religion, and the problem of providing a definition lies in the general and the particular. Religion is a very loose term, but we have a lot of very loose terms.

On the last day of class someone will usually raise a question that allows me to ask them if their understanding of the word religion is elastic enough to embrace all of these things they've been reading this semester, or have I asked them to read some things that they might think is not religion? And earlier, when discussing definition at the beginning of the class, I always remind them that definitions are defining words in terms of other words. They're not descriptions of things.

EUGENE GALLAGHER: Earlier in the conversation, you alluded to training graduate students to be teachers of undergraduates. Have you thought at all about what would be an appropriate way to train graduate students for entering into the undergraduate classroom?

JONATHAN Z. SMITH: We don't value apprenticeship much anymore in most trades and professions, so why is it the only mechanism we have in our profession for teaching graduate students to be teachers; an invitation and an apprenticeship—and it's all left as a fairly unreflective process.

We have a situation in which some professors are obviously quite good at teaching and a lot of us really aren't. But we don't have a general education on education. And what is more, we tend to disdain it. We say that teaching is all in the heart, and all that garbage. A particular professor is beloved by his students and it's because he tells jokes in class. There is actually an anti-education feeling among many educators. They don't want to be in the business of education.

I think one really has to break down the process of teaching. You can't do it in situ because everything comes at you all at once. You have to disaggregate. So let's talk about writing. Or, let's talk about problem-solving. Let's talk about different styles of learning, but let's also talk about the different styles of presenting. I'm very self-conscious about what style of presentation I'm using on any particular day—whether it's narrative mode or problematic mode, and so on. By the time the semester is through I've tried four or five styles for teaching.

There's so much good stuff written on teaching, and there are usually people on any campus who can talk intelligently about it. It's just unconscionable to simply throw the graduate students into the water with maybe just a seminar on teaching (which typically consists of a gripe session).

I've long advocated that part of a PhD requirement ought to be the preparation of a syllabus with a careful justification for everything included. Your degree should in large part depend on that. Yes, there should be a dissertation, but the rest should not be simply time served. And it's not enough to be just a teaching assistant in a class, because what you're really saying is thank goodness I had someone to grade all those papers for me. That's not sufficient preparation for a license to teach. What I'm asking for has to do with the ethos. When you put teaching in the graduate curriculum and you make it a degree requirement, then instantly we get serious about it. You take that away and it's simply a hobby. It's an avocation.

Everybody works out their own style eventually. But it's like improvisation in jazz: you have to improvise on something. And unless there's an agreed upon something I don't know how we evaluate it. I don't know how we write letters of recommendation. I don't know how we hire, and rehire. Well, I do know: the question of teaching just never comes up. I've never seen a hire which has requested a syllabus. You'd think it would be standard.

EUGENE GALLAGHER: At Connecticut College we've done that for a while now. Instead of teaching a sample class we ask you to bring a syllabus. And then we talk with you about it for an hour and a half. We ask job applicants to excavate the decision-making process in their syllabus, both pedagogically and in terms of field knowledge.

TIM JENSEN: That's something new at my university; all of us now have to provide a teaching portfolio. And every time we hire somebody, he or she has to produce several pages.

JONATHAN Z. SMITH: That's long overdue. I think it was at Princeton where they analyzed how faculty actually spend their time, and it's not spent writing books (which is what the dissertation is). We write articles; we give lectures; but we don't, on the whole, write books (and especially a book that's not simply a series of articles—which is what I do). So the dissertation is probably the last book you'll ever write, and it's advised by someone who has not written a book since their dissertation. This is a crazy system!

I like the idea that you should be able to give a popular lecture. You should be able to write a chapter for the Cambridge history of your subject—that is, a generalizing piece. You should be able to write an article that would be accepted by any refereed journal in your field. And you should have to present an annotated syllabus. All of these should be part of the PhD requirements. I think that unless we start putting some grit to this, it'll just be: nice guys think about teaching, and not nice guys don't. It becomes a moral statement, not a professional requirement. It's as if it's voluntary. I don't know any profession that lets you do that.

TIM JENSEN: Again, it's interesting that my context in Denmark is so different. I teach a required course each semester on the didactics of religion education or the didactics of the study of religions. So I have to teach methodology of teaching. How do you present this or that idea? What choices have you made? Why do you use this book instead of that book? This comes up all the time, because we are teaching this to our students. As part of the doctoral degree, students are required to write an essay that would appear in a popular magazine of some sort, and another essay that would be appropriate for an intellectual newspaper. Students are also required to analyze the issues that would come up if giving a television interview on, say, Shi'ite Islam or something like that. What topic would you pick? What's the important thing that you would want to say? And then reflect on how you as an academic differ from a journalist.

JONATHAN Z. SMITH: These kinds of exercises reflect the profession. It's what we do.

EUGENE GALLAGHER: Our job ads don't say: "Looking for person to write books on such and such," they say we are looking for a person to teach this, this, and this. And yet their training as graduate students is not all that well aligned with what they will be doing for us.

JONATHAN Z. SMITH: We have looked at it as a research degree and we have ignored the fact that it's also the credential in a teaching degree. The question is how much longer you can ignore that.

THOMAS PEARSON: We spend a lot of time teaching graduate students to do research and how to write. And yet they'll spend their careers teaching. So how do we teach them to teach? Have you ever worked with a graduate assistant who has watched you teach? Can you reflect on that process? Is that an effective method? How do you teach someone to teach?

JONATHAN Z. SMITH: Well, that's the apprenticeship model. It's one method, but I wouldn't want to make that the only method. It is partly imitation. That's how monkeys learn—so stop with the imitation already. But, let's be theological for a moment (although you hear this in the physics department too): it's charisma we're told. It's a gift. And some people have it and some people don't. The people who don't are probably pleased about that, by the way, because they don't get stuck with huge introductory courses. So it's one of the rare places where you'll hear faculty profess incompetence with great passion and great detail. It's a very strange thing we do by saying that teaching is an art—what we're really doing is saying it is not a profession. What we're really doing is denigrating it. I don't want an amateur to install my pacemaker and I don't want an amateur to teach me the Bible. It's just that simple.

So why is it that this enterprise of education, where ninety percent of the graduate students in any field are heading, is never discussed in a serious manner by most of the people who are training these people? For most of the institutions that are training graduate students, for most of the journals they would think of reading, this issue is not even on the radar screen. You can't blame the graduate students for this. There's no reason for them to have thought that education was what they were signing up for—although most of them are there because of a classroom experience that they had that led them to think that this is something they'd want to do with the rest of their lives. And we manage to pretty well freeze that out of them by the time they get through graduate school. That's just silly.

My wife is a professional musician, and she goes to conferences on pedagogy endlessly. Yes, you have to be able to play the piano and yes you have to be able to analyze the scores and do all of that. But what they seem to be going to meetings about all the time has to do with pedagogical aspects of their profession. And the sophistication of some of those pedagogical presentations is really quite stunning. Now, someone like Jerome Bruner[3] is a lot bigger in learning theory than I would like him to be but nonetheless that's a name that means a lot to any of my wife's colleagues. I bet you could walk around Swift Hall at the University of Chicago and no one would know who you're talking about. That's an illiteracy that is serious when you consider that this is what we get paid to do.

THOMAS PEARSON: So how does a graduate student learn to teach? Can you learn to teach by reading a book on teaching?

JONATHAN Z. SMITH: No, but it won't hurt you. That is, it will make you self-conscious. It will tell you things that you wouldn't have known because you haven't always been taught well yourself. Some of my colleagues spend hours grading papers and think they're being really good guys because they circle every mistake in grammar on the page—and we know that this sort of grading does nothing. It has no payoff. The kid glances at it once and goes on. The grammatical mistake continues. So even the people that you think of as spending a lot of time with their teaching, you have to ask: are their comments really useful? Do they know what kinds of comments might help? Do they know how to suggest a revision in a way that the student understands (that it's not that you change your idea, which is what they all take revision to be, but it's instead that you change how you said your idea)? There is a lot of good literature out there now on this sort of thing. I keep making that snotty remark that we ought to keep up with scholarship of teaching to the degree that we keep up with scholarship in our field—which to a certain degree is clearly hyperbolic. I surely don't keep up myself.

---

3. Ed. Note: Jerome Bruner, *The Process of Education* (Cambridge, MA: Harvard University Press, 1977); idem, *The Culture of Education* (Cambridge, MA: Harvard University Press, 1996).

But you should have some sense of what's out there. Because we do have this comforting illusion that some people are just naturally good teachers and some people are not. That lets me off the hook, and it's not true. I mean, there's a bit of truth in it, but not a lot.

EUGENE GALLAGHER: The further implication is that it therefore doesn't really matter much. It's not that important in comparison to your research profile. I think that's the profoundly damaging part given the economics of the industry and where people end up teaching.

JONATHAN Z. SMITH: And if they looked they would see that there is serious research on education, using methods they're familiar with, alluding to theoretical resources they're familiar with. There's no department more despised on any campus than its education department. I don't know of any profession that chooses to dump more garbage on its own profession than we do on education. They're the pariahs. We shut ours down at the University of Chicago. This is the tradition that goes back to Dewey. Do you think we need all that? I guess not. Benjamin Bloom's taxonomy of educational objectives is not considered a classic at this university. I have literally worn through a copy of Bloom.[4] I'm on my third. The idea that you could sit down and map out an intelligible language of what you wanted to do in a fifty minute class—I never knew you could really do that with his level of precision: "I'm going to target thus-and-so in the next class because look what happened Tuesday." Now, I don't necessarily hold out for everything in Bloom. It's like any taxonomy. But I don't think the notion of teaching as an art allows for there being that kind of taxonomy. It's as if we went "oooh" and "awww" over the smell of a tulip, but never knew what genus and species the tulip was. And again, that's so counter to the way we act with respect to almost anything else in our field. On the other hand, I will interrupt my class plans for a good newspaper article—what I call a gift from above. I think using the newspaper is important for a number of reasons. It puts the students and me on the same footing because we're both reading the same story at the same time—so it's not as though I've studied this text before. My article on Jonestown came out of a class like this.[5] Another example was

---

4. Ed. Note: Benjamin S. Bloom, *Taxonomy of Educational Objectives*, Book 1: *Cognitive Domain* (New York: Longman, 1984).

5. Ed. Note: Jonathan Z. Smith, "The Devil in Mr. Jones," in Smith, *Imagining Religion*, 102–20.

the Iranian hostage crisis. How could I hold class without reading what the students are reading in the paper about this? Our first presupposition was that the Ayatollah isn't crazy. He's rational. So he knows he can't win. So the question is how can he lose with the best face? One kid sticks up a hand and says, "Maybe it could be like Jesus"—and I was ready to kill him. But he meant to suggest that maybe there is some sort of special religious day on which the authorities could release the prisoners and save face—like Pilate in the Bible. The students did some research, but they couldn't find such a day. But I said, let's stick with that idea. If they did have a day such as that, what day would they pick? And they did some more research and decided that they'd pick Martyrdom. That's not bad, I thought. And it happens to also fit with the date of the crisis, and so forth, and it happened to work out. My students figured out the eventual date of the release. They were off by a day only because the banks had trouble transferring some cash and so they had to delay the release for twenty-four hours (and this changed the symbolism entirely, because it was Reagan and no longer Carter who was in office by the time the release took place). The timing of the release switched from a religious to a western secular calendar.

They figured this all out by themselves. They learned a few Arabic terms. They went and pulled down books from the library shelves. And they read with one particular question in mind, this goofy idea about a date on which prisoners could be released without losing face, like in the Bible. I wouldn't have expected that if my life depended on it. The students actually had three or four other theories going as well.

THOMAS PEARSON: It's problem-based learning.

JONATHAN Z. SMITH: Yes. And off they went.

THOMAS PEARSON: And it prepares them for how they're going to encounter religious discourses for the rest of their lives. They're not going to be reading myths throughout their adult lives, but they will be reading newspaper articles. They're learning how to interpret media.

EUGENE GALLAGHER: Which also just happens to be what the institutions that they're spending all this money at are promising they will be able to do.

JONATHAN Z. SMITH: I find newspapers very valuable in teaching. *The New York Times* had a story on a Tuesday about the weeping statue of the Madonna in a Catholic Church. On Wednesday, a Ganesh was leaking milk from his nipples in a temple. I brought this into class and asked students to compare how the *Times* handled the two stories. The first thing students noticed was that the tears were coming from an "icon" of the Madonna and the milk was coming from an "idol" of Ganesh. That was worth the whole day's discussion, how just a little change in a word could make such a big difference.

TIM JENSEN: Exactly. The didactics of religion and the study of religion should include the coverage of religion in the media. The words they use. How religions are represented. It's so important.

JONATHAN Z. SMITH: I find the newspaper very important because usually it is so un-self-conscious about these things. It doesn't know those words have a history.

[Doorbell rings. Jonathan Z. Smith stands and walks across the room to peer out the window but does not open the door.]

JONATHAN Z. SMITH: Hah! It's Jehovah's Witnesses. That's our data at the door.

[Laughter.]

SATOKO FUJIWARA: Do you ever take your students outside of the classroom, like to museums and such?

JONATHAN Z. SMITH: No, it's not in the schedule. I will call their attention to things that are happening on campus or in the community. I think I've always slighted the whole visual world, and I don't think that's a plus. I think that's a minus. Honestly, I don't know how to do it without it getting awfully like show-and-tell. I'm sure there are ways to do it. I've heard people do it successfully. But it's not my style. I'm not a very visual guy. I rarely go to an art museum, but I go to a book every day. That's what I do. But I do think it's a loss.

TIM JENSEN: In Denmark we struggle with how to teach students to read and discuss difficult texts and also to expose them to actual lived religion, to do fieldwork and experience the sociology of religion. It's too much to cover. I think there is a drift toward emphasizing contemporary religion and contemporary issues. The classic texts and the virtues of reading a text and studying religions of the past are being lost. I would like to return to an earlier point. When it comes to striking this balance between de-familiarization and familiarization—to challenge students without discouraging them or causing them to lose interest—there is also the problem of students having too much interest (in a sense) because they are relating to the course material as a Christian, or as a Jew. How do you handle that? Have you had to remind someone that they are here in the classroom as students?—that their comments are disruptive and are not the business that we are about here?

JONATHAN Z. SMITH: Yes, but I don't do it in front of the class. Except there was this one time when a student brought her minister to class to exorcise me, because she had told him that I was the devil. I came into class and there he was, this adult sitting amongst the students. He didn't have a collar on or anything, so I had to ask who he was and why he was there. It was explained to me and I said: "Now let's understand something here"—and I put it into language that he would understand—"In this classroom I am God, and no one comes in here unless I invite them. Now, if you would like to demonstrate what an exorcism is when we come to our unit on ritual later in the semester, I will invite you to come do what you're suggesting. But for now, you can get the hell out of here."

But that was the only time I've ever had a real chin-to-chin confrontation. After class I called up the counselors to tell them that I was a little worried about a student who was interpreting things in my classroom as the work of the devil. But more often I have students who get on a theme and can't get off of it. Actually, classmates usually do a pretty good job at stopping it, complaining that it's wasting their time. Just on economic grounds, they will not stand for too much of that sort of personal testimony. If a student comes to see me I will listen to a good bit of their testimonial and religious search and try my best to answer using the language that they themselves are using, if I can. I try to pick up some of what they say and reconfigure it and hand it back to them. But to me, that's an extra-curricular business. I assume that they know that if they come to a place like the University of Chicago that they really haven't signed on for that kind of affirmation of their religious experience. Since the George W. Bush administration I've found that I need to take a little time to make it clear that we are talking about religion, not faith. Certainly faith is an element in religion, but you can go a long way describing and analyzing what's going on in religion before you have to use the word faith. So you shouldn't start there.

EUGENE GALLAGHER: Again, when preparing graduate students to teach, you have to remember that you are sending them out into a very different context than they will have experienced at the University of Chicago.

JONATHAN Z. SMITH: I've never taught in an explicitly religious context. Other than Chicago, I've also taught in a state school, which was much more diverse than the University of Chicago (and probably still is). I think the smallest class I taught there had a hundred and fifty students—so whatever was on their minds would have been very difficult to tell.

I once taught a course with close to a thousand students and it was like being on an EKG. The sound that a thousand people make squirming in their seats when they're bored is like a slow rumble coming at you. Every sentence I muttered was monitored. I could tell if the rumbling started to get off of the idea. Time to do something else! Tell a joke. Do something! It just comes roaring up at you.

But I'm really not convinced that class size is necessarily as defeating as some people think it is. Certainly it takes a lot of work. I had a group of teaching assistants, but I was present at every discussion section. Clearly, I can't hear a thousand voices and I can't read a thousand essays, but there are some things you can do and there are some things that won't work in a large state university context. I remember my wife and I invited one of these large classes over to our house (not a thousand, but a class of maybe eighty-five or ninety). I'll never make the mistake again of setting out all the glasses I thought we'd need. Only one kid showed and we had eighty-five glasses sitting there on the table and this huge tub of beer and so forth. And there I was with this one kid who really thought he had to stay for a long time, I guess, and help me out a little bit—a little therapy for the old man.

In the first few pages of the new book I've just published (2012)[6] I say something about the importance of predictability when meeting with students. You should never cancel office hours. My students always know that I eat lunch before their class, in the same place. And I have a cup of coffee afterward. So they know where they can find me. But don't be disappointed if nobody shows up because adolescents have

---

6. Ed. Note: Lehrich, ed. *On Teaching Religion*.

many other things on their minds besides you and your stupid course. What free time they have they will not necessarily want to spend with you. But just because they haven't shown for weeks and weeks, you shouldn't give it up. If you're still there, some will eventually come by. At UC Santa Barbara we had only about one quarter of a table, but I ate lunch in the student cafeteria every day and there would be a shifting group of maybe forty students or so. That was more than enough. Not everyone has to come.

THOMAS PEARSON: Do you ever go to student functions? Do you go see what they get involved in?

JONATHAN Z. SMITH: I don't on the whole. I don't really see that as part of the job description. If a student organization asks me to come, I try to if I possibly can. But I want their effort to be in the classroom and on the books. And it's hard because students really don't expect or allow you to have a whole lot else on your mind other than your subject matter. After hours I'd rather talk about politics than sit around and talk about religion, frankly. But they don't allow me to have anything else on my mind. You can see that they've worked hard beforehand to think of something to say. "Let's ask him this." I just find that sort of thing stilted. It's easier at the graduate level because then you're in the same business so you can talk shop—formally, or informally.

THOMAS PEARSON: You've been teaching now for quite a long time. Have you noticed any change in the students over that period?

JONATHAN Z. SMITH: There hasn't been anything dramatic, I'd say. Certainly the student population is much more diverse now. That's been a change I've noticed at University of Chicago. Student diversity was one of the things I loved at UC Santa Barbara. I'm sure it's even more diverse now. When I first came to University of Chicago we had feeder schools and a fairly predictable student body. Now we have the problem that our undergraduate college is so much smaller than our graduate and professional programs. Most schools here run their college supported by graduate programs. Our college doesn't generate enough income to support itself so that's always a problem. You can get a lot of money from central administration if you can increase the size of the class. The unintended effect of this is that the students have gotten increasingly diverse, not just in their demographic profiles but also in terms of their interests and career plans and the types of educational experiences they've had. Close to a quarter of the college class thought of a career in the academy when I first came here. An awful lot of them were professors' kids. That's all gone now. Certainly by all the usual demographic measures the student body is clearly more diverse because going on to higher education has been more diversified. I don't think the institution can take any credit for that.

I wonder, and I wish I knew, what difference has been made by the ubiquitous use of computers. Nobody writes by hand anymore in class, they just type away. I wish I knew enough about computers to know what difference it makes, but I have never used a computer myself. I still refuse. So I don't have any real feel for it. Are things different when you have those sorts of tools available to you? Is it different when you can look up all this unmediated information on the internet? Students quote it to me from Wikipedia and I just shrug. But they know they're right and I'm wrong. One kid warned me that he was checking up to see if I had said things right. I told him that if it's that easy to find the right thing why do you bother coming to me? What are you putting me and you through all this for?

But I'm sure there must be a difference. I xerox all my readings, and the University wants me to put them on computers instead. But I won't do it. To me that's an insult to those texts. But I know you can provide things like visual art much more readily without having to bring in the slide projectors and all of that.

TIM JENSEN: [laughing] I'm looking forward to your next PowerPoint presentation.

JONATHAN Z. SMITH: That will be the day. I finally learned what it was! I had a vision that THIS was PowerPoint, [gestures emphatically with the middle digit of his hand, to laughter]. In the sciences now that's what they do. They all sit in the room together and look at the screen.

EUGENE GALLAGHER: While they read the screen out loud to them.

JONATHAN Z. SMITH: They don't even bother. They all just sit there and read it. Sooner or later this computer business has got to have made a difference. The authority of print has clearly been eroded in the minds of students. I've noticed that it is somehow rude to be critical toward a person, but it's okay to be critical toward a book. There's an etiquette involved, and there's so much now about making public what is personal. I think we're going to run into difficulty on this sooner or later. We may get a peculiar bifurcation whereby if you say it I won't analyze it, but if you have it set in lead, then I will. If it's flickering on a screen, then I won't. It may be like the suspension of disbelief in the theater. We may come to a point where we have genres that we will not or maybe ought not employ in certain forms. I don't know.

THOMAS PEARSON: Do you find that in the classroom the students are reticent to criticize each other's statements, because they are more critical of the text than they are of each other?

JONATHAN Z. SMITH: They don't like to criticize each other and they rarely do. If they do, it's allegorical. They'll address a point as if it was vaguely out there somewhere in the world and they're actually talking to the person sitting right next to them. Rarely is it face-to-face. I rarely teach a class that is small enough to be called a seminar, but generally at the University of Chicago a seminar is not a dialogue but a set of ejaculations. And, of course, a couple of people will consume most of the time of the seminar. So unless you're a traffic cop, not a lot of folks get to talk.

When I teach a large class of over a hundred students I take five minutes at the end of class and have them write a brief note to tell me the most surprising thing they learned that day and what they want to learn more about. They write that and hand it in and then I take five minutes at the beginning of the next class to report back what people have said and use that somehow in the class.

When I have a class of about thirty or so I set up a rotating set of designated discussants. Three designated students and I will conduct the discussion of the book. The next time around it's another three up there with me. They are the surrogates. I find that I get more out of them than if it was just left to them to stick up their hand and chime in. Everyone benefits more. And they're told to interrupt me. They don't have to put up their hand; they're supposed to jump right in if they need to. It legitimates for all the students that they could do this too. They don't, but they could in principle.

THOMAS PEARSON: Then do you grade them on how well they do?

JONATHAN Z. SMITH: No. The only thing they get that would affect their grade is if they don't do it at all, or if, on handing in written questions, they do not return them in a timely manner. The idea is that they know in advance so it's not a surprise. The schedule is known in the second week of class because by then the circulators have settled down and it holds for the quarter.

EUGENE GALLAGHER: So they get a couple chances?

JONATHAN Z. SMITH: It depends on the size of the class. They usually get two shots at it. I have to say that it improves the second time around. That's good to see. They are more forthright with me and they're more interesting about the text. They're taking charge of the discussion more and moving beyond being simply exegetical. Any kid with half a brain can ask you an exegetical question: "Would you say a little more about . . . this?" Which is what most class discussion questions tend to be—because they get credit simply for being active in class, you see. But with my system they know their turn is coming and some of them come in with notes. I can see if they are really prepared for this or not. And sometimes they think I don't ask the right questions. Every now and then I see some rumpling of papers in disgust. I want them to understand that not all speech is spontaneous and that spontaneity does not necessarily guarantee authenticity. They really do believe that.

THOMAS PEARSON: Well, thank you Jonathan, I think we're coming to the end of our time. I understand that this will be your last year teaching. I'm curious what you're going to miss the most about it.

JONATHAN Z. SMITH: Oh, I think everything. It's kept me on my toes for a lot of years. But it's gotten to the point where it's too much. I can't do the logistics anymore. My wife has to get me there and pick me up afterward. I think I'm probably getting a little tired too. I think I've done a lot more repeating of classes in the last several years. It used to be that at the end of the last class session I would stand up and walk over to the wastebasket and throw away my notes on the way out of the room. That way I would be forced to redo the class for next year even if the reading list was the same. A class should not be a trip down memory lane. So I would dump the notes and some kid would grab them up. I've noticed the last couple of years that I have revised but not destroyed my notes at the end of class, and that's a sign to me that I'm not quite as raring-to-go or as fired up as I was. It's time. I'm seventy-four years old, and you used to have to get out of the business at sixty-eight. So I figured I went a little longer than I had to, and that's enough.

I think I'll spend most of my time reading books that are not about religion. The third floor of my house is devoted to the books on religion; the second and first floor are lined with books that have nothing to do with religion. They're all novels or poetry. I think I read three of those for every book on religion.

The Dean's Craft of Teaching Seminar (2013)

As described on their website (https://divinity.uchicago.edu/craft-teaching) the Craft of Teaching seminar series is the University of Chicago Divinity School's program of pedagogical development for its graduate students, dedicated to preparing a new generation of accomplished educators in the field of religious studies. They bring together Divinity School faculty, current students, and an extensive alumni network of decorated teachers to share the craft of teaching and to advance critical reflection on religious studies pedagogy. On February 27, 2013, Jonathan Z. Smith was their guest, introduced by the then Dean of the Divinity School, Margaret Mitchell. His talk (which was accompanied by a sample syllabus that had been pre-distributed to the graduate students in attendance), approximately forty minutes in length, was following by a question and answer period of about the same length.

DEAN MARGARET MITCHELL: It's a distinct pleasure and honor to introduce our speaker this afternoon. I'm extremely grateful that Professor Jonathan Z. Smith accepted my invitation to come and give the Craft of Teaching Seminar. Jonathan Z. Smith is the Robert O. Anderson Distinguished Service Professor of the Humanities, also on the Committees on the Ancient Mediterranean World, on the History of Culture, and the College, associate faculty in the Divinity School in the area of the History of Religions. Jonathan Z. Smith is one of the foremost students of religion in our day—[turning to Smith] that's what you said, one night at dinner, you said "I prefer the title 'student of religion'." Am I right?

JONATHAN Z. SMITH: Oh, I was worried I said "the foremost." [Laughter]

DEAN MARGARET MITCHELL: Jonathan Z. Smith says he is *a* student of religion. I say he is a foremost student of religion in our day; I hope the air footnotes are clear.

Jonathan Z. Smith's impact on the guild of religious studies—through his insistence on care with terms, such as religion, demons, and others, his concern with proper methodology, especially on the nature of a good, responsible, and fruitful comparison, and on conceptual apparatus for our field or fields, in particular the use of taxonomy taken from the natural sciences—in all of these things his impact has been simply enormous. A magnificent essayist, with the keenest possible eye for a great topic and for interconnections, Professor Smith is the author of books you all have read: *Map is Not Territory, Imagining Religion: From Babylon to Jonestown, To Take Place: Toward Theory in Ritual, Drudgery Divine: On the Comparison of Early Christianity to the Religions of Late Antiquity*, and *Relating Religion: Essays in the Study of Religion*. This past year (2012), the volume of essays by Professor Smith, *On Teaching Religion*, edited by his former student, Christopher Lehrich, has appeared from Oxford University Press. Among others [included in that volume] is a classic essay that, I think, many here have read and it's also on our website, among others: "Religious Studies: Whither (Wither) and Why?"

If I could say just one personal note: when I came to graduate study in religion I had been a high school teacher for three years. And what it means to be a high school teacher is basically to be taught how to teach in survey mode, to move very rapidly over a series of topics. I had just finished my doctoral exams and I first heard Professor Smith on why survey teaching is deeply problematic and why it is far better to teach students to read one text deeply, thoroughly and well. And from there they can gain exportable skills for a lifetime of learning. I don't know if Jonathan knows that, but that's been formative for my own pedagogy throughout my career, as I continue to think about what it means to teach and to learn.

So without further ado I would ask all of you, here at Swift Hall today, to join me in welcoming Professor Jonathan Z. Smith.

JONATHAN Z. SMITH: Well, thank you. I think I'll start by just saying something about syllabi, since I was asked to supply one; presumably that's something on your mind. I'm just old enough to have gone to college when you got two things from your professor: you got a syllabus and you got a reading list. Those are not the same things; they now are. The syllabus is an outline of the argument of the course. You still get those in Europe. In fact, you can get a verbatim transcript of lectures sometimes as the syllabus for the course. Then there's a reading list. By putting them together I think we castrate both, but we're experts in hybrid genres nowadays. In my judgment, the syllabus is the most important piece of academic writing anyone does in the academic field. It's both a descriptive map of an area—as you see it, granted—it's both a descriptive map and an implicit, at least, argument. And I take it so seriously that, for me, it's the first primary text that we read together in class. It's what the first day of class is spent on; it's the first topic of discussion that first day of class, in which I try to account for the decisions I've made, from what I didn't do and for what I did, for why I think—but they'll have to decide that—there was a gain to the judgments that I underwent, so that I try to expose a syllabus as an implied argument, something worth thinking about. In particular, with this hybrid form, what was included and what was excluded.

Now obviously much depends on the type of course. I've been privileged since I've been here not only to teach for a while at the graduate level here at the Divinity School, but for more than a decade now spending my time mostly teaching at the college. And there one can teach as part of a general education program, which I've done, in the social science core, and there the syllabus is collectively arrived at with no small weight of tradition behind it. In the winter one always reads Durkheim—what else would one read in the winter? [Laughter] I suggested Freud since it was hotter, but I didn't get anywhere with the weight of tradition. On the other hand, when I did two sets of courses that fulfilled the Western Civ requirement, Bible in Western Civilization—or Bibles, actually, since it had the Qur'an and other texts, the Book of Mormon—Bibles in Western Civilization but then Religions in Western Civilization, one was freer, but one was still bound by an overall pedagogical reason for the college to privilege a particular course such as a civilizational sequence. There are surveys in which subject matter governs what you do, normally picking an area. There are courses I teach that I call basic structures, picking one or another—or in the case of the introductory syllabus, giving them to you all once—but looking at topics such as myth, such as ritual, or a subset that I happily gave on folklore—a variety of topics. Classics in the study of religion, and there in particular you incarnate the single book on principle: you read one book cover to cover, and you read it together with a class. And then the reading courses, honors papers, occasionally now still dissertation advising and so on—a whole realm of arenas—and each one of which has not only its own rules, but its own expectations in which if you're not handing out a syllabus, you're preparing one mentally in your mind. Now, let me say that I was a little reluctant to send you a syllabus because I learned early on that nobody can teach someone else's syllabus. When I started teaching at the University of California Santa Barbara as an acting Assistant Professor step one, because I didn't have my dissertation completed—in those days you could get a job without one—but the pressure was on. Finally—it's the only time in fifty years that I've taken one—I was given a leave for a quarter to finish the damned dissertation. I was supposed to teach a course called Introduction to the New Testament—a fairly standard affair—and they hired a graduate student of Dieter Betz from Claremont to come and substitute for me. And since his name happened to be Smith, the jerk simply handed out my syllabus. And I got this desperate phone call after about the third week: he said, "You know, your syllabus makes absolutely no sense to me. I don't understand why we're reading this passage in Paul, and that passage in Mark, and this passage . . ." I said, "Well why would you do that?!" And he said, "Well it was your course, so I thought I'd teach it." Well, I learned nobody can do that. So you take this only, please, as a very rough sketch, not any sort of sensible model to be emulated.

A syllabus gives you a course title, and to me that's always been the first object of interrogation. It's easier if the topic is Introduction to the New Testament—at least you can waggle one at them—harder if it's Introduction to Religion because I haven't the foggiest idea what you'd waggle at them. And so you start your opening sentences, at least to me, to introduce the complexity that will bug us the entire course, and will continue to bug us when we're finished, if I've done my job right. What is this an introduction to, religion?, religions?, The study of religion?—those are almost incompatible with one another. What is it that I am introducing? And that obviously raises the question of definition, with which we spend some time. Not only what is a definition—that wonderful phrase of Edward Bellamy: "It's enclosing the wild with a fence." That is the important thing, to me, about definitions: they limit. They're not generous, they're not "you all come"—that's what screws up most definitions of religion. You hear about some funny something or other and say, "Oh my god, I gotta change the definition to let

the Society of Boot-Strap Lickers and Worshipers into my definition." "No keep them out!" [Laughter] That's the job of definition: get as few things as possible on the table, but let them be the best examples of the species that you can get on the table.

So we spent time reading definitions. Dictionary definitions of two types: general lexical dictionaries, which my students learn never [to] accept if you're on the debating team—"quote Webster's, except to refute it." It says what everybody says the word means. And you're scholars now, and your job is *not* to use the word the way everybody uses it, but to use it for a particular purpose as a particular tool. So I don't want to hear about Webster's. So then the next thing we do is look at specialized dictionaries: dictionaries of religion. There, I must say, the definitions are even worse than Webster's, but at least they have some key words in there. They know the problem, they just refuse to speak to it. But that's then the topic, and that's what we're studying. We're going to try to define our subject matter—that's the way we introduce something. And that being said, I then shut up.

And the next thing the class does is take, in my kind of chronology, two cigarettes to write a definition of religion and, if they have time, of the study of religion, and I disappear and smoke my two cigarettes and come back in. And they've been told on the syllabus—because one of the thing I always do with college students is tell them the final exam on the first day of class so they can prepare—they know that their final paper, their only paper for the course, will be to revise that definition with specific reference to the materials we've read together in the course. So they begin to do what I began to do within the first fifteen minutes that we're together.

Then one has to decide, what can you get them to look at? And beyond the definitions, I want to give something that gives some sense of—I don't know what word to use—the *ethos* of the study of religion. So I picked two chronologically simultaneous, but attitudinally opposed documents: what I call The Emancipation Proclamation by the IAHR [International Association for the History of Religions[1]], in

---

1. Ed. Note: Smith points here to the so-called Marburg Declaration, issued during the Xth Congress of the International Association for the History of Religions, held in Marburg in 1960. Among many other statements, the Marburg Congress declared that "*Religionswissenschaft* [science of the study of religion] understands itself as a branch of the Humanities. It is an anthropological discipline, studying the religious phenomenon as a creature, feature and aspect of human culture." For more on this document, see the essays published, not long after the Congress, in *Numen* 7 (1960).

which, basically, a scholar is to check their religion on the coat rack on the way in the door: "It is the study of religion and we want no religious crap within the scholarly halls." And then the Supreme Court—the muddleheaded group of old farts [Laughter]—after coming out with their famous "You can't teach religion, you can only teach *about* religion under the Constitution,"[2] then spent basically most of the decision assuring everybody that they loved religion, was equally committed to it, America was religious, there was nothing better than religion, God save the Queen. . . . So two quite different arguments within which, I would say, you could divide the class: of those who are there because they are curious, but would probably hit you if you suggested they might be religious, and those who are religious, and wanted you to inquire further into their own tradition or find out why the other kind of folks are wrong.

So this gives them at least an articulate example of that argument, which is the repressed argument behind all arguments in the study of religion. It rears its head differently and under different disguises, but it remains. Then enough talking *about* it; we have to begin talk *with* it. And so the job, as you saw, was to have them read primary texts—fairly substantial primary texts—and one then needed a typology, the simplest typology I could pick up, it wasn't familiar—and there's an advantage at times to familiarity and at times to defamiliarization in the teaching of religion—was to make it [i.e., the type] vary by the social group. And so I had *traditional religion* (the polite word for "primitive") by which I meant religions that basically are ethnically constituted. You're born into it, and you can leave it but you actually can't leave it. But if you're outside, you can't come in it. That's a traditional religion. As goes the King so goes the country [is the] second category: *imperial religion*. And the third category, that which they've all defined for you already as what religion is: *associative religion*—individual matter, a matter of choice, a matter of inward disposition, a matter of faith, and all that other junk. So three types of religions, and we'll use those to organize the first part of the course.

Their own definitions were all associative; there wasn't an exception in the lot, regardless of the ethnicity and allegiance of the particular

---

2. Ed. Note: Smith refers to a U.S. Supreme Court decision (*School District of Abington Township, Pennsylvania v. Schempp*, 1963) in which the court ruled that officially or legally mandated prayer or Bible reading in public schools is unconstitutional.

student. It's been constant for the twelve-odd years I've had that particular exercise. One wants to insist, and therefore one has to lard one's examples with cases of it, that these are not three exclusive types. Very often one changes into the other, very often you'll find all of them simultaneously in any given culture, and so don't take them as hard-nosed categories but simply as a way of sorting the cards by suits early on in the game.

We began, then, with a set of texts in each case from a single cultural area—whether it's defined as a rather small area or a rather large area—and the job was to read, and I gave them the first example of the first one they had on traditional religions from Kalimantan (Borneo, in my day). And of course I picked it because, when I was young, "the wild-man of Borneo" was a trope you were all familiar with. Not only that, but you could go to any circus or sideshow and you could see one. Alas, it turns out, in most cases they are, in fact, autistic children who have been exposed by their parents for lucre. But nonetheless it was reported—by the way, and that was the first time I had actually thought about the wild-man of Borneo as opposed to hearing about them when I was a kid—it was reported that when [James G.] Frazer [1854–1941] was a kid, he was taken to see the wild-mannered Borneo and ran out screaming. And one rather psycho-analytically inclined scholar has argued that that's the source of Frazer's not only fascination, but this mania to prove that primitives are Ur-scientists, that there's rationality there, after all, that they weren't as frightening as little Jamie thought. [Laughter] I think that's crap, but that's the argument.

I took it because for me when I was a child the word Borneo meant not only a wild man, but Dayak went with head-hunting. There're over a hundred books entitled *The Head Hunters of Borneo* or *The Head Hunting Dayaks of Borneo*, and therefore they represent, in a way, "the most primitive of the primitive." And so they're a useful one to put on the table. Then, the best example that I know of is the work of [Hans] Schärer [1927–1997],[3] and that then raises several questions. First, the difference between, say, an ethnography—that is, *us* telling us what *they* think—and a primary text produced by the tradition where the tradition tells the members of the tradition what it thinks. And when you studied

---

3. Ed. Note: Schärer (1927–1997), who spent seven years as a missionary in southern Borneo (1932–1939), is the author of the 1946 book *Ngaju Religion: The Conception of God among a South Borneo People*, translated by Rodney Needham (The Hague: Martinus Nijhoff, 1963).

anthropological examples, you're often dealing with us speaking *for* them. So it's worth some reflection on that—it's worth some reflection to not only say the author is Hans Schärer but the author is The Very Reverend Hans Schärer, that is, he is a missionary. That doesn't automatically exclude him because it's usually the missionaries who have a consummate skill in the language, and that was the case. This was an oral culture, so he's produced the only Dayak text, until recent times. So it gave us a chance to talk about not only anthropology as an enterprise, or ethnography as an enterprise, but also the missionary as an enterprise. And there are places where he talks about their Supreme Being being the god-head—one suspects a bit of Germanic over-translation, when he has the tree of life in there (I'm not exactly sure, but I want to come back to that one, I'm not exactly sure that was their word for it). But on the whole, it's an important piece of work. What I also like is that in 1999, a very bright young anthropologist went and restudied this very group, so it's one of those rare cases where you can get an updated ethnography of the specific group as long as you don't poke someone else's territory, and so this was useful.

Then there was what you saw located in this book, my students had no knowledge of, and therefore not only located them on a map—where the hell they are—but located them in space and time, and that produced a rather long narrative in this case, but you would all, I suspect, have been able (as they, I suspect, were not) to decode what that was about. These are supremely historical people. They're not living in a vacuum. They have a history from the Stone Age to the present and have gone through a series of transformations and changes that absolutely boggle the imagination, including now declaring their religion a branch of Hinduism. So enormous, enormous change. Nobody is free from history—except maybe [Mircea] Eliade, but nobody else. Everyone else is embedded, up to their ears. Or, as I also teach my students, everybody came from someplace else and nobody is at home. And therefore, let's not make a deal about culture contact. You can't be in a culture without contact—they're synonymous terms. They're not something that happens to a subset of culture; they're part of the nature of culture.

So all of this gets talked about as we go through. In fact, since I'm usually long-winded, it's talked about a little longer than I'm talking about it right now. Secondly, however, this is their text, it's memorized, but we also have to be aware that these people's—most strongly in the

United States—traditional religions take advantage of anthropologists' labors. They now have printed text of their ritual. And so when this lady in 1999 interviews, as it happens, Schärer's prime informant (who is fortunately still alive), he's in the middle of telling her something and he stops and he can't remember the line—this is a text that takes some 18 hours to recite—he can't remember what line. He excuses himself, runs in, comes back with Schärer's book, which is printed in Dayak on one side of the page and German, which you can read, on the other side—finds the line, quotes it to her, happily puts it back, and continues with his eyes shut, beating the drum, to recite the text. Okay, so one is not only studying their religion, one is producing their bibles—one is producing their religious texts. Those green volumes that [Claude] Lévi-Strauss adores in the Bureau of American Ethnography are the prayer books of group after group after group in the United States who perform their rituals by the instructions written in the ethnographic reports.

This obviously is set up. If you look at the syllabus, the next thing we do is go to imperial religion, and we go to the loquacious Near East. Nobody scribbles as much as the Near East. And so you have the people who don't write and the people who write, and is that an important difference that is worth talking about? And the text we've chosen, in part, to allow you to see formulaic versus the oral, and to see references to other documents in the written and so on.

Now there is also built in here what I call "time bombs." I've left them in because they will lead some students to make mistakes, and since they write about each reading for me I'll find those mistakes and be able to work on them. For example—this one was innocent—I did not know on the front page of a handout that you read on traditional religions that this article on Peyote would produce such enormous indignation among my students. The notion that a religion would not let you in because you're not a Native American was absolutely horrific to them. I mean, you should have seen the indignation. And each time, there was practically a riot in the classroom that they read this thing they're furious about. That's how seriously we take the associative character of religion. "It's your choice; what do you mean it's their choice?" It's why Augusta can, until recently, not let women in.[4] In the eyes of

---

4. Ed. Note: The Augusta National Golf Club, located in Augusta, GA, and home of the famous annual Masters Tournament, admitted women into its membership only as recently as August 2012.

the Supreme Court, a religion is like a private club; it's allowed to exclude. That's the *Boy Scout* decision: it's allowed to exclude those who it wishes to exclude.[5] I don't particularly hold out for the genius of that argument, but let's let it roll. Anyway, I didn't expect that.

Second time bomb: I asked them right away, in fact after they've looked at this syllabus—I like Sam Gill's definition, which is why I chose to quote it—but "What would you revise in it on the basis of your reading?" What I hoped they would revise is the sentence that: "they were largely uninfluenced by the cultures of Europe and of Asia" because of the deep influence of both India and China upon the cultures of Borneo or Kalimantan were emphasized in the reading, and so on.

Third: And I don't know—as I can't read Ngaju—I don't know whether it is a proper translation or not but it doesn't matter for the point I want to make: there will always be eight or nine students absolutely thrilled to find a tree of life in a garden in the middle of this Ngaju text, and not only that, but man and woman are created next to that tree of life. And they're absolutely thrilled—there's nothing more exciting to a student. Most of us are attracted to the fields we're in because of the differences in religion; most of the college students are attracted to looking for similarities, and there's some sense of triumph: "See we influenced them too!" or something—I don't know what the hell it is. But they're all excited about it, and you stop and say, "Now just a goddamn minute. This is a tree with its roots—it's Eliade's tree—it's got its roots in the underworld and the crowns in the upper world, its trunk is in this world. It's not that dinky little Genesis tree—it's just a little old tree! This is—the Empire State building is dwarfed by Paris...."

Secondly, did you really pay attention? I know it's where they created man and woman, but *how* did they create man and woman? [Mutters representing students' lack of response.] No, no, come on, tell me! How the hell did they create man and woman? "Well you see, these two hornbills were fighting with one another—they're the Divinities, you know, Mr. Smith...." I said, "Oh, Jesus, we're really like Genesis

---

5. Ed. Note: This refers to the 5-4 U.S. Supreme Court decision in the case of *Boy Scouts of America et al. v. Dale*, 530 U.S. 640 (2000), in which the constitutional right to freely associate (understood, in U.S. law, as an aspect of the freedom of speech) was interpreted by the Justices as allowing private associations, such as the Boy Scouts of America, to exclude classes of people from membership in their organization.

now"—two hornbills are whacking at each other with their horns, and one accidentally knocks off a little bit of moss from the tree, and out of that males come. And the other one accidentally whacks off a little mushroom from the tree, and out of that female comes. I mean, we got a strong parallel there—I mean, I charge plagiarism. [Laughter] But I know they're going to fall for it every damn time, and so it's in there, in part, at least, for that sort of reason.

The second half [of the course]—I can be much, much briefer on this—the second half is the one that forces comparison. The first half I hope you'll compare between those three types [of religions], but nothing that I do makes it inescapable for you to do it. The second part of the course is constructed around fundamental structures in religion: myth, ritual, the sacred persons, and so on, rites of passage. And in each case, they have a set of reading of snippets, of small pieces of text drawn from all three religious types. So therefore, they can't talk with any authority about the culture and leave it all embedded there; they've got to compare through the different cultures. And what can they compare it to? The only thing possible is to the type. And so it gets them into that mode of reading.

Beyond that the only other thing—because I want to hear from you—that I want to say is that I chose for the Dayaks a very long text—it's about 50 pages. I, because I pay for this xeroxing, I reduce it down like this [shows condensed document], so it's five columns of miniscule writing, and there's about twelve to fourteen pages of this to read. I do this, in part, because right here [Smith displays page to audience] is Schärer's summary of the myth, of this whole huge thing. And I have them look at that because what I want to remind them of is that every anthropological convention [since] Lévi-Strauss, almost all myths you will ever read in texts that are not folkloristic or archival in nature, is that kind of summary. So when you read that kind of summary, that you read now in two minutes, behind it is this enormous thing that you've slugged through—if you've stuck with it—for hours, and it seems, to me, an important point to make.

So that's maybe, I think, all I want to say about the materials that you had a look at. . . . So let me hear from you, please.

DEAN MARGARET MITCHELL: Ok, the floor is open for questions and comments. Dive in.

STUDENT 1: Thank you, Professor Smith. I noticed you have not included different theoretical approaches. . . .

JONATHAN Z. SMITH: No, that's a separate enterprise. Can't do everything in one quarter.

STUDENT 1: You don't do this in the Intro to Religion class?

JONATHAN Z. SMITH: No. That's a choice one can make. That is, if I was teaching an introduction to the study of religion, I would focus on that.... By doing introduction to religion, which is how I understand this course, I review primary texts. I sneak in other people; they get a bibliography with each one of the topics, and I get to see names recurring. I'll say something about [Arnold] van Gennep on this, Eliade on that.... Bruce Lincoln is an example: Bruce on this one, and so on. But no, I don't think... if I have only one course to teach—and that's the way I look at this—it's one day in teaching time. It's less than a 24-hour day. I got one day, how am I gonna spend it? I rather would look at the stuff than look at the theories. I also teach courses on theories and I teach courses on individual theorists in the college. But that's not, to me, what you do the first time. For the majority of students this is their first and only course they're going to take in religion. Less than one day... Less than 24 hours they have.[6] So no, I don't do that except indirectly.

STUDENT 2: You said that by putting the book list and the syllabus together you "castrate them both." Can you say a little more about that, and what's a different way of presenting those two texts?

JONATHAN Z. SMITH: Yeah, I basically think one—I've got an example of it printed here—where you have the readings as one list, and that's the efficient list. And then you have statements—a little bit of what you've just heard from me—you have the statements about what the payoff of reading that is: what to look for? why is it important? what is it linked to? That is, you have a set of arguments, reflections on hoped-for results of the reading, so it's the logic of the reading, if you want, along with the reading. I find that if your syllabus gets overly long, it will not be looked at at all. So the combination means about a twelve-page document, and

---

6. Ed. Note: Smith here refers to the total number of hours, in the University of Chicago's ten-week quarter system, that students spend on one subject in one course. See Jonathan Z. Smith, "The Introductory Course: Less Is Better," in *Teaching the Introductory Course in Religious Studies: A Sourcebook*, ed. Mark Juergensmeyer (Atlanta: Scholars Press, 1991), 187.

they're not likely to look at it. So I think that's what happens. I myself wish we would go back to handing out two documents: the efficient document, if you want, for those who simply know what they're supposed to read for the next day, and a more "think piece-y" sort of document. I think it would be helpful. It's more helpful than those catalog descriptions.

STUDENT 3: I wanted to discuss the associative religion type that you were talking about. How do you handle situations where the student does come in—even in Judeo-Christian culture—and they come in with their own assumptions and presuppositions about religion and about biblical Judeo-Christian texts. And yet you bring up a different culture where there's a tree of life, and they impose their sort of bank of knowledge onto that and get excited about the similarities. How do you handle that kind of situation when people are already coming in with a predisposition about their own take on religion and then they impose it onto contexts outside of their own?

JONATHAN Z. SMITH: I mean, first of all, it seems to me that's not a peculiar problem to religions; any subject people come in with their own take. And I would say two or three quite different things: one, it's not always easy to find out about the take, so you have to try some multiple ways of finding it. Type of questions, writing on every assignment where sooner or later they're going to get really fatigued and tell me what's on their mind, and that's great help to me. But I don't think there's anything particularly special about that. And I don't think they're our jobs necessarily, by the way, to uproot that either. Our job is to say: But have you thought of this, have you thought of that. Someone else could take that symbol and see something very different in it—had you thought of that? Have some people in the tradition that you're familiar with—because I wouldn't want to eliminate the imagination of the people on the tree of life in Western tradition—have they come up with something like that? Damn yes, you do find cosmic trees, certainly in Romanian material, which Mircea [Eliade] hit us with all the time, so yeah. I don't think that's a special problem. I think it's a problem for you of your patience with it. And I mean that not because the subject makes you impatient, but because you hear it so many times and it's so god-damn unimaginative when you hear it. And you have to be, I think, patient with it. And you try to say: Look, eternal to any tradition, that's worth being called a tradition, is variation, disagreement, and so on. So multiple interpretations are present within any of those traditions, and I'm sure there's a point at which we can find the contact between some understanding over there and some understanding over here. What you don't want to do is draw global conclusions from that, you want to draw very modest conclusions from it. But the human imagination goes to work on these texts, these traditions, and not in radically different ways—different, but not *radically* different ways—it seems to me one sort of takes for granted.

STUDENT 4: I was wondering if you could talk a little bit, then, about what happens during the time the class meets for a class like this, especially since there are 142 students, so what happens during that time?

JONATHAN Z. SMITH: What happens during the class time is what happens to any course that I think of as an introduction, that is, I do a lot of talking. To me, an introduction has an introducer, and my job is to introduce. My job, secondly, is not to wait for the odd or assorted question. Often the nod is usually a reaction to something just said, which is not very helpful. But you have to find ways of instigating conversation. My way of instigating it is by getting those statements from them for every reading and getting it before the second session on that reading, which means I can say, "A number of you thought . . . and so would someone please explain that to me" or "You, Miss So-and-so, said . . . could you explain that to me? All right?" Or something of that sort. So that to me, the idea of having a weekly writing—outside of getting people in the habit of writing—is to give me some raw material to target the kinds of questions I'd like us to ask, which are not just some of the questions I'm going to get asked. Then one tries to be available before and after—they know where I am before, they know where I am after. There are other kinds of classes clearly—twelve of us sitting around the table reading [E. B.] Tylor—if we can stay awake—is a very different formula than this sort of thing.

STUDENT 5: I'm curious—there're only so many hours in a day, and there's not only the choice of what you teach, but who you teach. And I'm curious, as an educator, what do you feel are the benefits and drawbacks of teaching low-level undergraduates—or maybe just undergraduates in general—versus graduate students? What effect do you hope do have with them down the road, in terms of the big picture?

JONATHAN Z. SMITH: Well, I, in all due respect, have always been very clear about my choice, which is to teach college students and get them in the first two years. I'm not interested in majors—that already to me is the end. It's getting boring. And what I want is a few moments of their time so that, as they go on in the things that I can't even imagine, every now and then something will hit them, and then they'll give me another few moments of their time. I guess that's what I see it as. I don't want to train anybody for something. I really don't like that role—I play it, but I don't like it. I really want to enable interesting gossip. [Laughter] That's my idea. So I want them to have . . . fortunately, actually, religion is not a rare topic of conversation, so I'd like to have some impact on that conversation. That would make me very happy.

STUDENT 5: Just a follow-up, could you give a concrete success story, for example, of a student you've had as a low-level undergrad, or you've heard about something they've done, or you just thought that that was a great success story?

JONATHAN Z. SMITH: Yeah, I'll give you an example of a student I had from college through a PhD from the Divinity School, so many, many, many years [ago]. And she's now an expert in information retrieval. I don't even know what it is. I don't use a computer. I have no understanding of that world and wish not to have any understanding of that world. And she sends me her publications and I read them, faithfully. I don't have to know what the hell she's talking about. And I see, as I read them, suddenly: classification. A big deal about it. All into this stuff. And then she's talking at one point about comparison—she's not comparing anything I would compare, but she's comparing. And I see her talking about comparing is not just "like," comparing is. . . . We got somewhere. Thank you, Carol, it's been worth it. One of them makes it worth it, frankly. It's a very haphazard business. [Laughter] I mean, I describe it as shooting BBs into a bowl of jello. Sometimes there's resistance, and it stops. Most of the time it squirts right through. That's what it's like. So, a couple like that is enough to make it feel worthwhile. But that's what you're trying to do, I think: you're trying to inform general discourse. That's where I link education to civics and all of those other things. When I say it's a political act—by that, I don't mean what Bruce [Lincoln] means—I mean it's an act of making a decision, that the one thing we don't tolerate is no decision. The one thing I've said and the one thing I praise most—as someone predisposed not to praise it at all—about professional education, there's one thing it tells you is no matter how complex, you've got to reach a decision, and it trains you with a decision. Right? We can't have a surgeon up standing in the middle of things. And what ideally makes a decision is discourse, an intelligent discourse. So that's what I think is what one tries to do. I would gladly teach another subject—I have no particular investment in the subject I'm teaching, really. I might have been much happier teaching something else, but here's where I am. I'm not going to say "God help me, I can do it no longer." But here's where the dice got thrown. But it's okay because I would do the same thing in something that I feel more comfortable with.

STUDENT 6: You mentioned that part of your practice on the first day of class is to justify your syllabus by explaining what you've chosen to include and also what you've chosen to exclude. And I was wondering if you could say a little bit about what you take to be the excluded on this syllabus—like what you didn't include?

JONATHAN Z. SMITH: Theology is the biggest single exclusion. That is, I—and it's the failure of the course. To me, the most interesting part of religion is studying data and the reinterpretation of it. See that's where I have a field day with a year-long course on the bible because all I basically taught was reinterpretation, from Ur to the Book of Mormon, and I loved it.[7] I have not—and I tell the students this, it's the greatest single failure of this course—I'm going to tell you there were priests, but I'm not going to tell you their words. And it's that side of it: the updating of tradition, the working of tradition, the absorption of novelty, the saying you're saying the same thing when you're never saying the same thing—all of that. So the fakery of tradition and the genius of tradition. And that's the part I have to leave out; I can't see a way of sticking it in. I really can't. I've had—there are occasional readings, the one on the end of the world because it's interesting: everyone talks about myth and almost always wants to talk about the beginning of the world, and the end of the world is never one of the first things you tell me when you tell me what a myth is. And so I took the end of the world. And there you can pick up a little sense in the readings on that because—because [the book of] Daniel stands behind the Jewish, the Christian, and the Islamic passages we're reading—you can see Daniel rearing

---

7. Ed. Note: Ur, according to Genesis 11:31, was the hometown of the biblical Abraham.

his head out of the sea. In any . . . That's the only time where it comes up explicitly. So I think one of the things that keeps religion alive—and my language, who was lying about it?—that's what keeps it alive. "We've always believed . . . ," they say. (Oh yeah?). "We've never believed that . . ." (The hell you haven't.). But lying about it . . . "This is what this text means!" (No.) But that's the lifeblood of religion. So it changes all the time, and it would die rather than admit it changes. It's the only phenomenon I know that's quite like that. Most of the time we'd love to say we changed. Where would science be if we can't announce, "Oh, we used to think that; we don't think that anymore." Our sense is "We've always thought that!" Right? And that's the part I leave out. So to me, the dynamic of religion—I don't teach in *this* course. I over—I have to say, my students will tell you—I over-compensate for that in some of the other courses I teach. One student wrote in the evaluation for the bible course, "Isn't there anything but interpretation?" and I wrote, "No. [Laughter]. Not in this course." But that's the biggest thing we lack. And then we lack the sort of systematic articulation, unless you're comparing—that's what I meant by theology—unless you're willing to take a myth as in some sense a systematic interpretation—the problem is it's an implicit system and this is not the audience to get that implicit system out of the myth. So for me, what I really miss—and it bothers me but I don't know in one quarter, ten weeks, how to correct for it—is what I would call the thoughtful part of religion. It doesn't mean what we're looking at is the irrational part, it's not the "now I will sit down and think about this" side of it. And that is not there, in this course.

STUDENT 7: You can come up with such a well-crafted syllabus, I believe, at an early stage of your career and have great confidence in it. But when you're starting out as a scholar and that's . . . , you're teaching your first class and you don't have the breadth and depth and that confidence about it, how do you go about coming up with a syllabus, the first drafting, or choosing and excluding readings?

JONATHAN Z. SMITH: Actually, you should watch me do it because you wouldn't see a lot of confidence [laughter]—there's crumbled paper all over the floor. And I wrote a little piece, the opening piece of this [gestures to his book, *On Teaching Religion*], that I gave here at Swift Hall, on approaching the college classroom,[8] and said a little bit about

---

8. Ed. Note: See *On Teaching Religion*, 1–8.

the practical side of things, like keep notebooks—don't let any idea you have get lost—as soon as you finish, go back and revise—what worked, what didn't work, and so on. But that doesn't answer your question about how you do it the first time. You imitate. You imitate. You think of some class you've had where something worked, you think of something like that, something that worked in that class, and you build out from there. You ask advice. You go look at, you pull out the syllabi you have from other classes you've taken. There's no manual on how to write a syllabus. A syllabus is a funny thing, it's a very personal statement in a very formal format, so it's really an odd genre. I find it takes a lot of time. Even if I've taught the same, or roughly the same syllabus for years, I still have to think it through each year and go back over what worked, what didn't work, and decide if what didn't work was really fatal enough that I really need to change it. And that means that you keep a kind of a running diary of what you're doing. You don't let all of the work you put in go to waste. It does get easier because you slip into habit, and so it's very nice every now and then to have that habit destroyed, to do something different. I mean, it's very important to recover that insecurity. But I would say you have models, you've had things you've seen work and not work; you can come up with analogs to them. Of course, many teachers—not just beginning teachers—do the—well, go the road of scoundrels. I was trying to figure a nice word and I couldn't think of it. That is, they use a textbook. And of either kind: a textbook which is like me that just doesn't stop talking and talks its subject through or a reader, an anthology of some sorts, that someone else has made—and now what you have to do is retroactively be like that poor Mr. Smith who called me, "Why the hell did he put that reading in?" All right? But there is that other rubric. I don't like it because it seems to me your investment in that course is not there. I very much think of this as *my* course. I wouldn't like someone else to teach that syllabus. I was in a frightened notion that sometimes people are, but I wouldn't like somebody to. It's *mine*. Yet, I have to say I start off each year with a blank piece of paper, and think it through again. And there have been changes, over the years, in this thing....

I see a hand, I can't see who's with it, but there's a hand way in the back near a window.

STUDENT 8: I'm curious, because you've seem to have spoken very engagingly about a course that seems to be called 'Introduction to Religion' and yet the syllabus says "Introduction to Religious Studies."

JONATHAN Z. SMITH: Yeah, I can't help it. They gave me the title.

STUDENT 8: That's understandable, but is that something that you work in the course at all, that discussion?

JONATHAN Z. SMITH: I talk about the difference between them, yes. And tell them why *I* don't call the course that, but *they* call the course that. And since it fills a requirement, I guess I got to call the damn course that, too. And I think that's because the program is called Religious Studies, so this is now an introduction to, not just to the study of religion, but an introduction to a program called "Religious Studies." And I take it—that's the way I would defend the logic of it. But see, I get into your issue, if I really said this is course on the study of religion, then I'm flipped right away to the theoretical, to the methodological, and so on, and that's not what I wanted to do in this particular course.

STUDENT 9: Along a similar line, I appreciated your comments on never teaching somebody else's syllabus. What are some strategies for making a syllabus one's own if there are institutional expectations on not only title of the course, but on specific content, or on format of the course, that you're there to teach, especially as a new member of the faculty?

JONATHAN Z. SMITH: Bow down to the wind. [Laughter]. It's not worth the job. I certainly taught a course, my first teaching, with which I profoundly and utterly disagreed. I thought it was stupid. I still think it's stupid. The chair of the department also wrote the book we used which I think is stupid. And I crossed my fingers and taught it. Like a demon! [Laughter].

STUDENT 9: What was the course?

JONATHAN Z. SMITH: It was called "The Judeo-Christian Tradition." And I said, "The only interesting part of that title is the hyphen." [Laughter and applause.] I only said it the last day of class. "Folks, or gentlemen," since it was at Dartmouth, "we've spent a whole goddamn semester studying a hyphen. Have fun!" But that does happen, and if it does happen, it's not . . . come on. What I would say is that when they have those things—we have them here—and if they work, they're okay. And that is a course that really is a staff course. There're really a couple of people, or if someone of merit is rather big, then it's fifteen or twenty people. And in some sense that course is a reflective judgment. Now, as you could add to it, you've clearly got a template that's there, you could argue like hell to move a beloved reading, but you could make that argument. And I've seen them. I mean, I saw Vic Turner junked for Lévi-Strauss—Vic's a lot easier to teach. Boring in the long run, but a lot easier to teach. It's scaring the kids with Lévi-Strauss, but that's the way they wanted it. So I have no implicit objection to teaching in effect what's somebody else's syllabus, if it's collective and if we have a chance—this has a weekly staff meeting—in which we can all postmortem how it's working. And that's okay, it seems to me, even though, I admit, over the years that tends to get—to do something I don't usually like to use, but use the word "ritual" pejoratively—that tends to be an empty ritual. You gossip more than you fundamentally argue about the issues of interpretation of that passage in Freud. But I—yes, one, very often, is handed a syllabus, or one, very often, has a job which is a replacement, like this poor guy had. Sometimes you . . . yeah, I think, in principle, it doesn't work because I think so much of you is writ into those syllabi.

STUDENT 10: I have a question of how one deals with the medium of teaching, the fact that you're dealing with readings and discourse and you're talking about something that's practiced. How do you sort of bring that alive, despite that fact that you're giving it to your students on paper?

JONATHAN Z. SMITH: I can't. You can't. Movies don't work. I can only . . . I can only do it with off-hand remarks. But they've all seen ceremonial occasions, they've all seen ritual, they've all done these sorts of things. And so you just remind them that we're reading a third-hand description of something. There are people who are doing it first-hand. But short of that—but that, you see, it seems to me that dilemma is part of the dilemma of the study of religion. The study of religion presupposes some measure—we can argue about the yardage—but some measure of distance. And "some measure of distance" means it's not enabled, alive, and so forth, in front of you. It's not quite in a biologist's jug of formaldehyde, but it's closer to that than it is to living. Okay? Because we fixed it, and we fixed the moment of it. Or we fixed a very abstraction of it, which isn't even a moment of it, so that you can't really do that. And field trips and all that—we're in college now, not in high school anymore, so to hell with that. But many of them have a very keen sense of it, and again, they will talk about it, it will inform some of what they do, but I don't think we can do much more than that, myself, of course.

Now partly—that's my nature—I prefer to read above anything else in the world, and I don't want to experience, I want to read. I want to have experienced someone's experience that's printed. That's my idea of a hot time in the old town. [Laughter.] So I'm very comfortable with this dilemma, but I do recognize with my colleagues—especially some of my younger colleagues—the dilemma this has become, in fact, more of a front and center issue. When I was trained, one never read anybody who was alive. That was the first time you were a graduate student. Couldn't be alive—not that they'd be worth reading if they were alive. [Laughter.] Until moss is on the stone, they are not worth reading. Now I know experiential learning is a term of art, okay? So the world has turned, and I'm an old fogey . . . on that one . . . among others. [Laughs to himself.]

STUDENT 11: You mentioned that you assign weekly writing exercises, and then there's a final paper, and then you also have a journal?

JONATHAN Z. SMITH: No, what you're . . . I urge them to keep a reading journal. I don't see that. What I see is what I call "Questions and Observations on the Readings." And those are handed in to me. They're not graded—how the hell would I grade them?—the fact that they're handed in is graded, that is, I'll penalize you if you don't hand them in regularly and on time. And since I read them all, and I use them, and I construct what we do in class very much out of them—sometimes with named credit, sometimes without. I get that every week, so I get ten of those in the course of this course. And then their paper actually should be able to be written out of those, because the paper simply asks them to take, after all, to interpret something that they themselves wrote, but now evaluate it in light of the things that we have read. And so obviously, I mean . . . that religion is a matter of free choice is going to go from some people's definitions of religion—some people actually had it in the definition. . . . A lot of talk now, because it's in the news, about freedom of religion. And the idea that religion and freedom are inextricably melded together—which is, first of all, a very odd and peculiar idea given history, but one that I wouldn't liken to a definition of religion. Religion is freedom? Hell it is. It's coercion. But I hope they have a journal because I don't want them, for instance, to give me an outline of what they read—but it might not be a bad idea to try to make an outline—I don't necessarily want to hear that they think this text is boring and all that, but they may want to remind themselves never to read that damn thing again. So I'm perfectly happy that there be another mode of writing that I don't look at. You see . . . let me say this, because I've written about this, and to me it's the greatest problem a teacher faces. I know how a student *writes*, I don't know how they *read*. And I'm persuaded that if they read badly, they write badly. They read well, they sometimes write badly, too, but I don't know how they read. When I was younger and more ambitious, when I would teach in the Core, I'd call in their books—I'd have them give them to me, and I'd go home and study how they underlined. Fascinating, how they underlined, by the way. One who had a black schmearer and obliterated everything on that page she thought was not important. The only thing that was left was (wanted to be a doctor yet; scared the hell out of me) [laughter] . . . and I couldn't understand what she left—I think I wrote about this one[9]—she erased all of Durkheim's, just his opinion, and left only the facts: "The Australian eats an [inaudible]"—that was there. "This is a totem" [gestures erasing the Durkheim quote]—that was not. So, oh, just the facts ma'am was left. [Inaudible.] It was worth its weight in gold to find out that's how that soul was reading. So it's fascinating to me, but it also took an awful lot of time, particularly when you'd meet with one of them about the readings that they did. But it's a great frustration how they read. So anything that gives you a modest clue as to how they might be reading—here's someone who clearly is going to read for biblical parallels all the way through, so I better try to say something about that before this gets completely out of hand or someone else thinks that's a good idea since I'm not grading these things—I didn't say she was wrong.

STUDENT 12: Is it—and if it is, why is it—important for religion to be taught?

JONATHAN Z. SMITH: It's no more important than any other subject to be taught, but it's an active force in the world we live in and has been an active force in the world we inherited, and as such, is worth some thinking. I wouldn't make much more plea for it than that. It's got a place on the landscape—it's never been a minor place on the landscape. And so some knowledge of it . . . And I suppose I would want to say, in the context of education, some

---

9. Ed. Note: He gestures to *On Teaching Religion* beside him on the table, at this point, suggesting this is discussed in that volume.

knowledge, at least, that not everyone's [religion] works like the one you may be most familiar with. That there's difference and that's supportable, that's okay, I think is what's useful. . . . We've been through phases—it is interesting. Twenty years ago, my sense is, it was very much an antiquarian subject: you had to work as a teacher very hard to persuade people that religion was a visible part of the world we live in today. And that was part of your job as a teacher. But our job now is to shut the windows already: it's pouring at you from all over the place and it looks almost incomprehensible because there's so damn much of it. There's too much static. So now the job is, in a way, to try to not dwell on all the minutia but to step back a little bit from all of that. But the mood has certainly changed. Religion is a taken for granted topic, it seems to me, for most of our students today. I don't mean students in here, I mean students in the wider sense of the word. And I think it was very much *not* a taken for granted subject twenty years ago.

STUDENT 13: I was wondering if you could say more about your approach—approaches specific to discussion-based classes, whether general education classes or seminars on particular topics?

JONATHAN Z. SMITH: I've never trusted spontaneity, so there's always a designated person to start our conversation off, and I have to have someone out there I can count on who I know has read it—because it's the wrath of God that's going to get them if they haven't—and has come in with something prepared to set us off with. And so it's always been an instigated discussion, never a free for all. And I've done that in even some of the very large classes. In the Bible class, there would be a designated row, and I would pretend they were the only people in the class and I would talk to them, ask them questions. Next class, another people—another oct of ten—that's how you can take 150–200 students and still have one discussion with them. I learned that through a footnote in a horrible curriculum committee report—give credit where credit's due. I also had had another suggestion, which was another way of provoking discussion, which is to take five minutes at the end of each class to say "Write out for me what was the most interesting thing you learned today, and what do you wish we had discussed?" And start the next class by reflecting on those. I must say sometimes it blew my . . . sometimes they're fooling around: "Where do you buy your ties and who does your hair, Mr. Smith?" And, you know, "You're a nice teacher," so okay, ha ha [Laughter]—God forbid you're not, you know, one of the guys. But it settles down pretty fast, and the questions are extremely good. And so now I'm asking them their questions, I'm not asking them my questions, and that makes a big difference, by the way. And so I try to leave it not just to potluck. Once it gets going, it's potluck obviously, I mean, you can't sit there programming the thing. But for a core studies, primarily a discussion course, there's always a device of some sort because there are no such things as discussion classes. Every seminar I've ever observed as I've walked down the hall: there are four loudmouths and everyone else is quietly listening. There are four incompetent lecturers in every seminar class—that's what it is. And so you might as well spread the incompetence around, is my judgment, and make sure everyone gets a chance to be publicly incompetent.

STUDENT 13: I was also going to ask about your use of humor in your classes . . .

JONATHAN Z. SMITH: I try to be very serious all the time, I hope to God. [Swears on it by raising left hand and places right hand on heart] Did I put up the right hand, Elaine? No it's wrong—is this the right hand? [Corrects it and then salutes instead. Laughter] So help me God.

DEAN MARGARET MITCHELL: Well, I think that's a very good note to move the conversation over to refreshments. I think, among other things, you have enabled this group here to be much more interesting in their gossip about teaching of the study of religion. Please join me in thanking Professor Smith.

Essay

Reading Religion: A Life in Learning (2010)

INTRODUCTION
Ann Taves

When it came to choosing plenary speakers, there was no question in my mind as to whom I wanted to invite to give the "Lifetime of Learning Address." The address, modeled on the ACLS's Haskins Lecture, offers a speaker the chance to "reflect . . . on the motives, the chance determinations, the satisfactions (and dissatisfactions) of the life of learning . . . and to explore through [their] own life the larger, institutional life of scholarship.[1]

"Jonathan Z. Smith, the Robert O. Anderson Distinguished Service Professor of the Humanities at the University of Chicago, grew up in Manhattan where as a teenager he aspired to be an agrostologist, that is, a botanist who specializes in breeding grasses,[2] a plan he did not abandon until he belatedly turned to the study of religion and philosophy as an undergraduate. His early fascination with botanical classification, the Marxism of Manhattan's West Side, and Cassirer's work in linguistics all left their mark on a scholar who more than any other has shaped the study of religion for our generation.

Smith received his B.D. from Yale Divinity School and his Ph.D. from Yale's newly established Department of Religion, then taught at Dartmouth for a year, before joining the Department of Religious Studies at UC Santa Barbara in 1966. Two years later, he accepted the University of Chicago's offer of a joint appointment in the undergraduate College and the Divinity School,

---

1. Ed. Note: The following lecture, previously unpublished, along with Ann Taves's introduction (she was then the president of the AAR), were both part of Smith's "Lifetime of Learning Address" at the annual meeting of the American Academy of Religion (delivered in Atlanta, GA, on October 31, 2010).

2. Ed. Note: In person at this point, and off-mic, Smith added here, while wagging his finger at the audience: "When grass was just what cows ate."

entering into a relationship with the university that has now spanned over four decades. Grounded in the College both as a teacher of undergraduates and for a time as an administrator, his relationship with the Divinity School and with his senior colleague, Mircea Eliade, has been more complex. As he has acknowledged, much of his early scholarship was devoted to articulating both his respect for and dissent from positions taken by Eliade, who epitomized for many what it meant to be a historian of religions. A bit less obviously, we might add that much of his writing on early Christianity and early Judaism articulated a similarly complex relationship to the traditional divinity school curriculum.

So, it strikes me that Smith has not only tackled the central issues in the study of religion, he has also modeled how to engage respectfully with and at the same time dissent from that which we have inherited. Looking back, I think it is clear that the four moments, which he in time identified as central to the renewal of the comparative study of religion—description, comparison, redescription and rectification—were worked out not only in relation to two exemplary comparativists, first Frazer, in his dissertation, and then Eliade, but also in relation to an exemplary body of data, that of early Christianity, which lay at the heart of the divinity school curriculum and which, in that context, was assumed to be singular and incomparable.

In all cases, he has insisted that careful, respectful contextual description of an exemplum must precede the setting up of comparisons between exempla along lines of interest to us as scholars. The aim of the comparison is both to redescribe the exempla (each in light of the other) and to rectify the academic categories that have been used to imagine them. In Smith's hands, the comparative enterprise, thus, becomes an engine of change. What so many of us have found exhilarating in Smith's work, I think, is a procedure for taking the past seriously, treating it respectfully, and at the same time, in stressing our role in setting up comparisons, providing a means of rethinking the categories that have traditionally informed the study of religion.

All of which is to say, when it fell to me to select a scholar to give the Lifetime of Learning Address, it struck me that there was a gap, an incongruity, a somewhat unseemly difference in the level of appreciation shown to Smith by the organizations in which he has played such an outsized role. While Smith's role has been recognized by both NAASR and SBL,[3] both of

---

3. Ed. Note: These are two professional societies for scholars of religion: NAASR = the North American Association for the Study of Religion; SBL = Society of Biblical Literature.

which elected him as their president, he has not received the same level of formal recognition from the AAR, an oversight that I felt we clearly needed to rectify. So this lecture—titled "Reading Religion: A Life in Scholarship"—provides a way for the AAR to recognize and honor the central contribution that he has made to our field.

Please join me in welcoming Jonathan Z. Smith.

Well, thank you, Ann; I couldn't have said it better myself.

As Gérard Genette reminds us: within a written text, the prime function of an authorial preface is neither to claim truth nor accuracy in what follows, but rather sincerity. In pre-modern texts, a loose category that has increasingly become a major focus of my reading, such a claim is paradoxically made in an address to a reader—an oral form in a written text. The paradigm for this mini-genre remains [Michel de] Montaigne's "Au Lecteur," prefacing the initial 1580 printing of his essays: "Reader, this here is a book of good faith." By way of a prelude, I would proffer the same compact with you for the duration—but only for the duration—of this address.

I am far from insensible to the honor, interest, and yes, forbearance you have extended me by your invitation to speak with you on this occasion under the general rubric of a lifetime of learning address. I take some comfort from the implication of the first element in that assignment that the chief criterion for your selection is a measure of longevity, recalling that the first occasion at which I was invited to speak at a plenary session of our academy was Dallas forty-two years ago. Through many years of continued association, this academy has unfailingly gifted me, as it has so many others, with a sustained thoughtfulness as both a persistent presenter and auditor. The AAR has provided one of the essential formal and informal contexts for my ongoing work as it has for so many, many other scholars.

Now, by way of a further relaxation of my charge, I note that the gerundive "learning" suggests an ongoing process rather than an attained achievement—an inference I underscored by the prepositional revision of my subtitle "A Life *in* Learning." The knowledges, you've been informed at this academy series, was modeled on the fabled Charles Homer Haskins lectures, sponsored by the American Council of Learned

Societies—the ACLS—did little to alleviate my initial anxieties. The ACLS asks each speaker—and you've heard part of this—to reflect on a lifetime of scholarship, on the motives, the chance determinations, the satisfactions and dissatisfactions of a lifetime of learning, and to explore through one's own life the larger institutional life of scholarship. Our president, Ann Taves, after quoting the ACLS charge to me, made clear, with characteristic gentle steel, that I was held to the same agendum. It's a daunting prospect; it suggests on such an occasion one makes of oneself what is more appropriately—and surely more comfortably—an undertaking for others. The thought that the vagrant details of one's life story and career might be taken in some fashion to be typical, even exemplary—and I use both of these latter terms in their strictly taxonomic sense. Besides, it has been my experience, inasmuch as scholarship is both a communal and communicative enterprise, perhaps better realized in the traditive processes of teaching than in the substantive ones of publication, that more often than not, the published collections of scholars' correspondence are better at revealing the tenor of their thought and practice than are the autobiographies by the very same figures. Think in this context of the case of two scholars, who find a place on my list of patron saints: Wilhelm von Humboldt and Sigmund Freud. Besides I remain ever mindful of the quite proper critique pressed by the now old new criticism as to the relevance of the biographical to an understanding of the product of a life's work. For this reason, my epigraph to this morning's text is [Friedrich] Nietzsche's caution to his readers in *Ecce Homo*: "I am one thing, my writings are another."

These, along with similar hesitations and scruples, were, in some measure, relaxed by a phrase in the already quoted ACLS description of the Haskins Lecture: "The chance determinations." This provides something of an escape clause—one that was notably seized upon and exploited with his characteristic rhetorical genius by Clifford Geertz in his 1999 Haskins Lecture, "Passage and Accident."[4] As you've just heard, beginning already with the second term in his title and continuing throughout, Geertz carefully crafts an aura of contingency for his bios. From his opening sentence, "It is a shakening business to stand up in public towards the end of an improvised life and call it learned," to this description of his career: "As in probably and casually as we [that is Hildred and Clifford

---

4. Ed. Note: This lecture is available as chapter 1 of Geertz's *Available Light: Anthropological Reflections on Philosophical Topics* (Princeton, NJ: Princeton University Press, 2000).

Geertz] had become anthropologists, just about as innocently, we became Indonesianists, and so it goes, the rest is post-script: the working out of a happenstance fate."

If I were to make a list of the chance determinations that will touch my narrative this morning, leading obscurely, and far from inevitably, to my standing before you on this occasion, they would have to include from my pre-professional history, and without elaborating details, being placed at Haverford College, an institution I had not previously heard of, and after encountering, accidentally, one teacher there my first week, becoming a philosophy major rather than concentrating in biology as planned. That professor's joke in college that led to my going on to Yale Divinity School, as well as the new context there spurred by a Supreme Court decision that led to my abandoning a thesis in New Testament in Early Christian Literature and writing, instead, the school's first dissertation in History of Religions. As I had already attempted in my bio-bibliographic essay "When the Chips are Down" in *Relating Religion*,[5] both to describe my most central and persistent scholarly preoccupations and to relate those to a number of my publications, it seemed appropriate not to rehearse that account or to attempt its like here today. Further, I shall take a somewhat different tack, yet one I believe consonant with my assignment; despite no small degree of wincing on my part, this will at first require several youthful anecdotes, but not too many. In obedience to Benjamin Disraeli's witty wordplay in his overlong satiric 1890 novel *Lothair*, that when a man falls into his anecdotage, it was a sign for him to retire.

As I began to draft this presentation, I sought some red thread that might establish path-marks through what seemed to me to be a labyrinth of accidents. Its initial point, I quickly divined, would surely have to be my sheer love of words. I love hearing them, speaking them, above all, reading them, not so much writing them, but reading with considerable speed and concentration resulting in ready memorization—characteristics exhibited since pre-grade school days. I have been told that my early formula, "Reading makes me eat," resulted in my mother sitting by my highchair or small table reading aloud to me through every meal hour. As she had scant patience with children's literature, she read to me systematically, volume by bloody volume, from a set of the collected

---

5. Ed. Note: Smith is referring to his own essay collection *Relating Religion: Essays in the Study of Religion* (Chicago: University of Chicago Press, 2004).

works of Charles Dickens. This precocious verbal diet no doubt accounts for my early and still continuing adoration of reading dictionaries—first for unknown words or usages encountered that day, and then, I admit, a page or two for the sheer pleasure of it. When I had graduated to an abridged Webster's by the time I had entered a first grade class at PS 9 in Manhattan, this fact, uncovered and then verified by my teacher during the first week, led to my immediate transfer to something called Hunter College Elementary School, a public school administered by the New York City Board of Higher Education. Individual work was there emphasized, and I indulged freely in my love of words, leaving the classroom to spend most of the time in the school's well equipped library, later in Hunter College's library, the 42nd Street Main Public Library, and most beloved of all, the library of the American Museum of Natural History, which lay on my bus route home from school.

At eight or nine, during summer day camp, I recall my thrill upon learning a mock-heroic doggerel fireside song, "Abdul Abulbul Amir."[6] Its twelfth verse, well into the description of the *mano a mano* combat between Abdul and Ivan Skavinsky Skavar reports:

> They parried and thrust,
> they side-stepped and cussed,
> of blood they spilled a great part;
> the philologist blokes,
> who seldom crack jokes,
> say that hash was first made on that spot.

"Philologists," back then, was a brand new word to me. I guessed from its two elements that it had something to do with a love of study or words, although, upon returning home that day, my dictionary stressed its reference to an academic discipline that studied language, labeling a lover of speech as being obsolete. Never mind. What delight to finally have a

---

6. Ed. Note: the later song was based on a poem written in 1877 (at the time of the Russian-Turkish war) by the Irish writer William Percy French (1854–1920); the poem's first stanza opens:

> The sons of the Prophet are brave men and bold
> And quite unaccustomed to fear,
> But the bravest by far in the ranks of the Shah,
> Was Abdul Abulbul Amir.

twenty-dollar word for my passion. Many years later, I had an occasion—I fail to remember why—to read in Martianus Capella's prolix early fifth-century allegory, *The Wedding of Philology and Mercury*, and found there the term's widest application as an emblem of the totality of the liberal arts. But at that early a time, the term finally gave me an answer to that persistent, utterly premature adult's question:

> And what do you want to be when you grow up?
> A philologist, sir![7]

It says something about the way I read at eight or nine, that I was puzzled by the plot of that banal campfire song, narrating a duel to the mutual death between Abdul, the son of a prophet, a bold *mamluk*[8]—I had to look up that word, also—and Ivan, a bold Russian who fought in the ranks of the Tsar. Where, I asked myself, in the sands of Arabia—where, thanks to motion pictures I had, until then, imagined Islam—would those two have encountered each other? After some library times, several encyclopedia articles and book chapters later, I'd learned much about the expansion of Islam in the thirteenth through seventeenth centuries, the Ottoman armies, the Russian conflicts of the mid-sixteenth century, and the Crimean and Caucasus, the so-called Long Wars, and so forth. This made plausible the song's duel, but my view of world history as an essentially interactive network and the Eurasian continent as a single unit was first formed back then, by that stupid ditty, remaining largely intact to this day, especially in the 1980s and 90s when I came to design and teach several new versions of Western Civilization courses both for the college and the School of Continuing Education at the University of Chicago.

Now, as for becoming a philologian in the lexical sense, to my chagrin, I found the learning of others' languages extraordinarily difficult. I think I spoke and read so fast that it seemed a degradation to go back and learn to read or say, haltingly, sentences the equivalent of: "It's raining outside. Where is my umbrella?" It was only in graduate school, when with fellowship monies, I could afford to hire tutors to teach me to read a particular book I desperately wanted to study that was not available to me in either English or French, that I was able to gain some ability

---

7. Ed. Note: at this point in his address, Smith adds as an aside: "Agrostologist is just as bad."

8. Ed. Note: based on an Arabic word for property, implying a slave, but of a warrior class, evident across parts of the Muslim world, from the ninth century onwards.

to read, although never to speak, a number of other languages. Hunter College Elementary School, by emphasizing individual work by arranging for tutorials on any subject that might have interested you, was, as well, the beginning of a curricular ideal in student practice that continues to this day. My conviction that, beyond the necessary introductory courses, learning best occurs in guided reading and independent studies. The firm belief that no topic is so jejune that with proper guidance it will not exfoliate into a web of associated areas, disciplines, and sorts of knowledge.

As an example of the idea in mind, I recall, in the tense period of Berkeley's time of troubles in the [19]60s, being put on a University of California, Santa Barbara, curriculum reform committee charged with thinking about an Honors College. I argued that each student should be asked for at least one academic year—I lost—to explore a topic encapsulated in a single sentence, following out its implications and wherever *it* and *their minds* might lead them. My example—admittedly, designed to provoke—was a quotation from General John Pershing's report to the Secretary of War.[9] As quoted in a 1915 address to the Tenth Annual Rotary Convention, by Charles E. Barker, an officer in that association, and later reprinted by him in a sex education pamphlet distributed by the University Society entitled *What Fathers Should Tell Their Sons*—the second half was *What Mothers Should Tell Their Daughters* by a different author.[10] Pershing's statement reads:

> I am proud, as the American commander, to say that I have personally investigated the rosters of some of the regiments of the American soldiers overseas. Thirty-six hundred strong—battle strong—regiments, and there isn't one case of venereal disease among some regiments who went over.

Now, I suggested to my colleagues that beginning with the question of credibility—and while we're on the topic, how many were "some"?—exploration of this passage might lead one to the study of epidemiology,

---

9. Ed. Note: John J. Pershing (1860–1948) was a noted US military figure who played a prominent leadership role in the U.S. involvement in the First World War.

10. Ed. Note: What was then known as a doctor of hygiene and physical culture, Barker's 1915 lecture (delivered in Salt Lake City, Utah) was entitled "A Father's Responsibility to His Son"; although many editions exist of the book that subsequently resulted, Smith is likely referring to the 1919 edition published in New York by the University Society.

statistics, the history of popular American moral discourse, propaganda in World War I, questions of national stereotypes, to suggest but a few. It will not, I suspect, have escaped those of you who have read me that an analogous procedure underlies the bulk of my published work: the unpacking of a simple, single example, an e.g., through a dense fabric of associations and implications.

My facility in and fascination with the act of reading brought with it a host of auxiliary issues wrestled with particularly in high school and college. I had a capacious memory, but required a more secure mode of memorialization. Back in those days, prior—believe it or not—to both inexpensive paperbacks and photocopying, besides the second-hand copies I was beginning to acquire on Manhattan's fabled 4th Avenue booksellers row, my reading was necessarily in library copies, often in non-circulating titles restricted to reading rooms. To mark or otherwise to deface *them* seemed to me to be, at the very least, a mortal sin. I worked through a variety of genres of extraction from miscellanies of common place books, outlines and sheets of topically organized citations, to carefully constructed digests and abstracts—the latter device I still use and rely on today.

The other major problem, typical of an autodidact, was the happenstance character of my reading: Something caught my eye, I'd use a reference work to make an initial reconnaissance and bibliography, and then read whatever became at hand. In an attempt to be more systematic, in 1952 I purchased a paperback copy of *Good Reading: A Guide To the World's Best Books*, edited by the Committee on College Reading, and set out through my high school years to read my way through the listed titles, category by category. By the summer of 1956, I had read some three-quarters of the recommended works. In both college and graduate school, my reading, fortunately, necessarily became relatively more focused and surely directed. I developed a set of reading rules for myself—still followed—that I printed in "When the Chips are Down."[11] When initially drafting this presentation then, I experimented with a

---

11. Ed. Note: See *Relating Religion* 31, n. 27, where Smith writes as follows: "I developed a set of reading rules I have followed ever since. These include: always read the entire chapter of a book in which a reference you are looking for occurs, then read at least the first and last chapters; always skim the entire volume of a journal in which you are seeking a particular article, then read the tables of contents for the entire run of the journal; after locating a particular volume on the shelves, always skim five volumes to the left and to the right of it; always trace citations in a footnote back to their original sources.... Later, I added: do not teach or discuss a figure unless you have read the total corpus of their work that is available to you."

number of titles, each reflecting the interests I've just narrated, and therefore, each containing the word "words." Jean-Paul Sartre, in his autobiographical account of his childhood, had already appropriated the bluntest candidate, *les mots*, "the words." But beyond a reluctance to imitate him, Sartre's sense of "words" as articulated therein, was too materialistic, too bound to things for my more idealist taste, and so I feared your misunderstanding. I was briefly intrigued with the title of N. Scott Momaday's collection *The Man Made of Words*,[12] but seemed, even for me, pretentious as a self-appellation. I was more tempted by the image of a web of words, a possible etymologically-influenced translation of the word "text." The phrase already occurs in the third millennium B.C. Sumerian Kesh Temple Hymn as a spinning of the writing goddess Nidaba. Then, too, I recalled, my outrage, preserved in a college-era commonplace book with C. G. Jung's dismissive use of the formulation. He writes:

> No one can really understand these things unless he has experienced them himself. I am therefore much more interested in pointing out the possible ways than in devising intellectual formulae, which for lack of experience, must necessarily remain an empty web of words.[13]

And after writing out the quotation, I angrily scrawled, "Nonsense,"—it was a blunted term—"with this he has abdicated his right to be taken, in any way, seriously as an intellectual figure." But beyond my fear that my use of "web" would suggest a change of heart, in my thorough distaste for all things digital, I did not wish to infringe on the intellectual property of the author of the canonical use of the term. K. M. E. Murray's magnificent biography of her grandfather, *Caught in a Web of Words: James Murray and the Oxford English Dictionary*, a man who was, for me, a hero and whose life's work has been a daily companion for decades. Besides, one of the first pieces of Mircea Eliade that I had read, "The 'God who Binds'

---

12. Ed. Note: N. Scott Momady, *The Man Made of Words: Essays, Stories, Passages* (New York: St. Martin's Press, 1997).

13. Ed. Note: The quote from Jung—the noted mid-twentieth-century psychologist and one-time colleague of Freud's—can be found in his essay "Individuation," in the concluding lines of the section entitled "Anima and Animus"; see p. 211 of his *Two Essays in Analytic Philosophy*, translated by Gerhard Adler and R. F. C. Hull (Princeton, NJ: Princeton University Press, 1972).

and the Symbolism of Knots,"[14] had alerted me to the complex multivalence of binding, knotting, and netting imagery. I therefore settled for the far more prosaic and British academic sounding formulation, "Reading Religion." Not alone because it continues a fondness for gerundive titles, but because it is, in fact, the most accurate description of my primary work as a student of religion, of what I do day to day. I intend the conjunction to distance myself from other possibilities, most particularly that advocated by Jung and by some of our colleagues: experiencing religion. My scruples are, perhaps, overly developed in this regard. I've been long fond of a work by John Capgrave, Provincial of the British Mendicant Order of the Austin Friars centered at Lynn. In his official capacity, he journeyed to Rome in 1450 and wrote an account of sites seen, "The Solace of Pilgrims." It opens with a twofold claim of veracity: "I shall not write but that I find in authors or else that I see with eye." Throughout my career, it has been my bias to affirm the first, the authors, and to utterly dismiss the second: with mine own eye.

Through the years, my chief mode of travel has been to go to the library or to my bookshelves. Although I've written a good bit about place, I've never had the slightest desire to see for myself the places I've described. I've relied, rather, on published sources, photographs, sketches, verbal descriptions, maps, diagrams. Once, with Elaine, by accident, I found myself before an unknown, rather confusing building in the old city in Jerusalem. When told that it was, in fact, the Church of the Holy Sepulcher, a site to which I had devoted a chapter of a book, I went no further inside remarking, "I prefer my church to theirs."[15] This is to say—and I'm serious about this—this is to say, as I wrote in the conclusion of "When the Chips are Down," I have consistently made a choice of the *map* over the *territory*.[16] Although you may well disagree, it has been a self-limitation that, for me, yields cognitive gain. That is, reading as a privileged mode of *mediated* rather than of *immediate* sight or experience.

---

14. Ed. Note: See chapter 3 of Eliade's *Images and Symbols: Studies in Religious Symbolism*, translated by Philip Mairet (Princeton, NJ: Princeton University Press, 1961).

15. Ed. Note: The church is said to be the site of Jesus's crucifixion, burial, and resurrection.

16. Ed. Note: The phrase is credited by Smith to Alfred Korzybski (1879–1950), and provided the title of Smith's 1974 essay "Map Is Not Territory"—a chapter in Smith's essay collection by the same name (Leiden: Brill, 1978). The concluding line of that essay reads as follows: "We need to reflect on and play with the necessary incongruity of our maps before we set out on a voyage of discovery to chart the worlds of other men. For the dictum of Alfred Korzybski is inescapable: 'Map is not territory'—but maps are all we possess" (309).

This is foregrounded throughout my published works, since 1966, with my characteristic deployment of the lengthy footnote, going far beyond mere citation of authorities—a practice that strives to fulfill the maxim proposed by the old Isaac Disraeli: "Digressions are never more agreeable than when they become dissertations."[17]—an aesthetic that accounts for my delight in reading and re-reading both [Laurence] Sterne's [*The Life and Opinions of*] *Tristram Shandy, [Gentleman]* and [James George] Frazer's *The Golden Bough*, two works I conjoined in my dissertation, as well as reading any number of digressive contemporary experimental novels.[18]

It was [Edward] Gibbon's [*The History of the*] *Decline and Fall [of the Roman Empire]* that first brought my awareness of this small paratextual footnoting genre. I know that I first used it in a junior high school history paper proposing a Marxist critique of automation—a precursor, I now realize, of my present disaffection with the computer. It contained nearly 700 notes: some simply a reference, but no small percentage extending over multiple single-spaced typed pages. To my chagrin, my teacher returned it with but a single comment, scrawled in obvious annoyance, with a thick carpenter's pencil: "Notes are *only* for citing the source of a *direct* quotation." I continue to resist that council of ignorance as I eschew the so-called—and equally ignorant—social science footnote format, which encourages that teacher's point of view. For me, a footnote is least interesting when it authorizes; it is at its best when it exposes, explores, and perhaps, mediates, conflicts of interpretations; for me, the chief goal of scholarship.

I was raised in a family embarrassed by the continued presence of religion—most especially, religious ritual—in their contemporary world. Religion was understood by them, and therefore by me, to be quintessentially irrational, although often fascinating as a funny instance of social or individual pathology. It was to be taken in the sense of one of my favorite grade-school books and newspaper columns, Robert Ripley's *Believe It or Not!*, whose paperback collection of what he calls "Queeriosities" begins

---

17. Ed. Note: The quotation, which concerns D'Israeli's assessment of Sir Walter Raleigh's *The History of the World* (1614), comes from an essay in volume 2 of the former's *Amenities of Literature, Consisting of Sketches and Characters of English Literature* (1842), entitled "The Psychological History of Raleigh."

18. Ed. Note: Smith's unpublished Yale PhD dissertation (from 1969) was entitled "The Glory, Jest, and Riddle: James George Frazer and *The Golden Bough*."

with a preface entitled "An Odyssey of Oddities"—he does have a certain sense of words. It's second paragraph opens with the dictum

> Strange is man when he seeks after his gods; therefore, the strangest places on earth are the holiest.

What follows is a largely accurate, sixteen page ethnographic description devoted to rituals preformed by the River Ganges, but framed by Ripley's relentless incredulity. While I might have initially accepted that perspective, I rapidly turned to seeking its mitigation, striving even as a teen—in what I would later come to recognize as being then, in a sort of free thought, rationalizing fashion—to uncover in religious items some kernel of possible sense. This culminated when I was twelve or thirteen with an attempt to rewrite a good bit of the biblical narratives so as to make them plausible. (I've learned since that that would be a great disadvantage.) From this small, rather naïve beginning, it later became the animating drive of my studies. Already to the fore as a college philosophy major to argue for, to hopefully demonstrate, largely through the interpretation of texts, the thoughtfulness of religion, and most particularly of ritual. In undertaking a variety of projects to this end, I took as my motto a phrase from [Sigmund] Freud but reversed his valence: That of the omnipotence of thought, the only god, I suppose, I recognize.[19] Freud had understood the term since his analysis of the "Rat Man" to be a negative characteristic of magical animism.[20]

By contrast, I took this as a positive goal, worthy of demonstration, coming finally to the view that the basic elements of religion are to be understood as strategies for dealing with a situation, as thoughtful exercises

---

19. Ed. Note: The phrase occurs in the title to chapter 3 of *Totem and Taboo* (1918): "Animism, Magic and the Omnipotence of Thought"; Freud writes in the opening to section 3 of that chapter: "I have adopted the term 'Omnipotence of Thought' from a highly intelligent man, a former sufferer from compulsion neurosis, who, after being cured through psychoanalytic treatment, was able to demonstrate his efficiency and good sense. He had coined this phrase to designate all those peculiar and uncanny occurrences which seemed to pursue him just as they pursue others afflicted with his malady. Thus if he happened to think of a person, he was actually confronted with this person as if he had conjured him up; if he inquired suddenly about the state of health of an acquaintance whom he had long missed he was sure to hear that this acquaintance had just died, so that he could believe that the deceased had drawn his attention to himself by telepathic means. . . ."

20. Ed. Note: "Rat man" was a code name Freud used for a patient he treated who suffered from obsessional neurosis (some of which involved rats)—possibly the only of his patients for whom notes on his sessions still exist due to their publication, in Germany, in 1909.

in human ingenuity. There is a sentence attributed to W. V. Quine, which that distinguished philosopher does not remember making, but said on hearing it that he would not disown it. It reads: "There are two reasons why a person is attracted to philosophy: One because he is interested in philosophy and the other because he is interested in the history of philosophy." Quine, as was generally characteristic of the analytic philosophers of the time, with important exceptions such as [Gilbert] Ryle, was uninterested in the second. By contrast, rather than philosophizing, the history of philosophy was my passion. But as a graduate student, I shifted to a focus on the history of religion. I first took it improperly to be analogous to the history of philosophy, that is a history of thinkings about religion—it's anything but—and made that my chief work. For example, my dissertation on Frazer's *Golden Bough*, had the form encapsulated in the titles of several books of the 80s: "Reading so-and-so Reading." The preparation for the Frazer work was reading every item cited in the footnotes of his third edition. The study was centered on what he made of them—his re-reading practices, if you wish. The same preparations and procedures have remained central strategies in most of my investigations of specific figures and schools of thought, as well as providing the background out of which I teach the same.

An equally dominant stratagem common to my interpretative essays of myths, rituals, and other basic elements of religion, attempts to limb out the situation, provoking and worked with, in the given basic element or religious tradition being studied. This may run the range from *intra*-cultural issues posed by the group's internal social logic to external problems raised by instances of *inter*-cultural conjunction. In another set, the focus has been on the problematics of difference, a question preoccupying my writings on comparison.[21] While the central topic here has been that of cultural and academic understandings, this has been extended especially in my teaching to other matters, for example, interpreting with a class variations in a given mythic narrative as instances of what I have come to term "thinking with stories." The procedure throughout these three foci remain that already described: to begin with a striking example, less commonly with a juxtaposition of two examples, in the service of the overall project of discerning and understanding how these give rise to thought—in them and for us.

---

21. Ed. Note: Smith discusses what he terms his career's "persistent preoccupations" in more detail in his essay, "When the Chips Are Down" (*Relating Religion* [2004]: 11ff.).

As with any sort of mythic discourse, I'm aware that my presentation has largely been a recital of elements of a story of origins—although unlike myth, one of an individual's formation rather than a corporate one. This seemed appropriate inasmuch as one aspect of my tale has had to do with improvisation. Many teachers, later colleagues, and students have been influential on my work—especially in its formative years—but always more by way of indirection. At Haverford [College] I focused on religion at a time when there was no program in the study of religion either at the college or at neighboring Bryn Mawr. At Yale I had the same good fortune: I became their first degree candidate in the History of Religions at a time when there was neither faculty nor a field so designated. The emblem for these changes at both institutions, establishing such programs (as well as others, although itself but one element in an exceedingly complex nexus) was, of course, the 1963 United States Supreme Court decision in *Abington v. Schempp*, with its legal and rhetorical legitimation of the history of religions, of teaching *about*—as distinguished from the teaching *of*—religion in public education.[22] The chartering of the American Academy of Religion one year after Abington, February 14, 1964, reflected the same nexus.[23] While one

---

22. Ed. Note: This U.S. Supreme Court decision, in which the Schempp family sued the Abington School District (in Pennsylvania), concerned the constitutionality of public schools engaging in/requiring prayer and Bible (i.e., scripture) readings as part of their daily opening exercises. The Justices, in an 8 to 1 ruling, declared the practice unconstitutional inasmuch as it was understood to contravene the Establishment Clause of the First Amendment to the U.S. Constitution (which forbids the government from making a law "respecting the establishment of religion")—a ruling that, though contested by some, stands to this day. Concerning Smith's comments on how the case was then used by some scholars to legitimize the field, the majority decision, written by Justice Clark, famously read:

> [I]t might well be said that one's education is not complete without a study of comparative religion or the history of religion and its relationship to the advancement of civilization. It certainly may be said that the Bible is worthy of study for its literary and historic qualities. Nothing we have said here indicates that such study of the Bible or of religion, when presented objectively as part of a secular program of education, may not be effected consistently with the First Amendment. But the exercises here do not fall into those categories. They are religious exercises, required by the States in violation of the command of the First Amendment that the Government maintain strict neutrality, neither aiding nor opposing religion. (See p. 374 U.S. 225 of the decision)

23. Ed. Note: The AAR—headquartered in Atlanta, Georgia, and the largest professional society in the U.S. for scholars of religion—developed directly from a name change of the National Association of Bible Instructors (NABI—which also means prophet in Hebrew; in 1922 it grew out of what had been known as the Association of Bible Instructions, founded in 1909), whose journal (*Journal of the National Association of Biblical Instructors*, founded in 1933), was retitled *Journal of the American Academy of Religion* in 1966. The Society of Biblical Literature (SBL—of which Smith was president in 2008), then seen as the more scholarly of the two societies, has existed since 1880 and, after a brief separation in the mid-2000s, the

may have wished for a set of more sophisticated formulations, this court decision enabled a new range of institutional forces, including—bluntly—many new employment possibilities. For example, according to an authoritative contemporary survey, there were twenty-five programs in religious studies, including denominationally funded ones, at public colleges and universities in 1960, three years prior to *Abington*. In the second edition of the same survey in 1967, four years *after Abington*, there were 135. The groundwork, it seemed to me, *then* was there laid for the development of a generic study of *religion*, but that expectation has largely remained unrealized. We seem still committed to the priority of species over genera, apparently confident that a focus on the former is the route to a responsible consideration of the latter without, however, much reflection on how one sort of expertise might, in fact, lead to the other.[24] I recall giving an opening plenary address, at Jim Wiggins' invitation,[25] to this academy some twenty years ago, in which I *gently* chided it for a then recent survey giving multiple options for the members' chief field of interest, thereby requiring someone like myself to write in, under the category "Other," "the study of religion." We largely train our students, and behave ourselves, as if the study of a particular religious tradition, always along with its attended philologies, is our vocation, as if generalization, comparison, or theorizing are but occasional avocations. I know, for example, how and where one gets trained, tested, and certified in another's language within our academic settings, but where is the space for gaining analogous competence in the second-order discourse of our field—in that which, among other possibilities, grounds efforts at comparison and at translation, be those narrowly or broadly conceived?

Now please do not misunderstand me: Linguistic ability of the first sort has become one of the crowning achievements of our field in the last decade—without it we would have remained but gossips. Sadly, we

---

two organizations collaborate on their annual conferences. The degree to which the theological (specifically Christian) roots of the AAR have been surpassed continues to be a point of debate in the field.

24. Ed. Note: Another way to phrase Smith's point might be to cite the general lack of interest among the majority of current scholars with studies of religion (in the singular), understood as a human phenomenon, especially with studies that apply explanatory tools from the social and natural sciences, in order to account for the tendency to be religious, while also noting the obvious wealth of so-called area studies in the field, devoted to studying the history or features of the religions in the plural, such as Hinduism, Jainism, Islam, Judaism, etc.

25. Ed. Note: A specialist in the history of Christianity and longtime Syracuse University faculty member, Wiggins was the executive director of the AAR from 1983 to 1992.

have not, however, had a comparable training or valuing of the second sort. Improvisation, auto-didacticism, with respect to the latter, are possible tracks for individuals; they have characterized a good bit of my life in scholarship, but such activities doth not a field of inquiry make. As Stephen Toulmin, seconded with uncommon eloquence by the late beloved Walter Capps,[26] remind us: such a field is not so much defined by its subject matter as it is by its keen awareness of a cumulative, second-order tradition of shared problems, interpretative and explanatory techniques and aspirations, as well as by the collective consciousness of its intellectual lineage of accumulated experience working with the same—an awareness largely gained by reading and thinking religion.

These are matters that those of us who now remain from my academic generation must now entrust to the rest of you in the hope that you will come to speech whereof we have all too often remained silent.

Thank you.

---

26. Ed. Note: The former was a British moral philosopher (1922–2009), and the latter (1934–1997) was a scholar of religion at the University of California, Santa Barbara, elected to the U.S. Congress in 1996.

Index

"Abdul Abulbul Amir" song, 116
accident. *See* chance
agri-business, 23
agriculture school, 5, 46
   elementary corn development, 5
Ainu bear festival, 49
American Academy of Religion (AAR),
   xii, 50, 111n1, 125, 125n23
American Council of Learned Societies
   (ACLS), 111, 114
   Haskins Lecture, 111, 114
American Museum of Natural
   History, 116
American Society for the Prevention
   of Cruelty to Animals
   (ASPCA), 8
Americanists, 59
anecdotes, telling
   sign of old age, 115
anthropology, x, 42, 47, 53, 59, 92
   ethnography, 91
   exotic right next door, 59
   of religion, 7
   speaking for others, 92
   studying urban populations, 59
   we produce their bibles, 93
Arabic, 77
Augusta National Golf Club, 93
   excluding women, 93n4
authenticity, ix-x

authority, 27
   of print declined, 82
avocation vs. vocation, 68
Ayatollah Khomeini, 77

Babylonian Talmud, 18
Barker, Charles E., 118
belief, 4, 15, 52
   distinguished from culture, 10–11
   signifying religion, 10–11
Bellamy, Edward, 88
Benney, Alfred F., 29–44
Bernard, Claude, 14–15
Betz, Dieter, 88
Bhagavad Gita, 17
bible, 7
   first claimed as inerrant, 9
   reading to start public school day (*see*
      Supreme Court of the United
      States)
biology, 50, 104, 115
   botany, 46
Bloom, Benjamin, 76
   taxonomy of educational
      objectives, 76
Bok, Derek, 10
Book of Mormon, 7, 14, 87, 100
Booth, Wayne, 19
Bornet, Philippe, 45–61
Boy Scouts of America, 94, 94n5

Bruner, Jerome, 75
Bryn Mawr, 125
Buddhism, 29
    suffering in, 34
Bush, President George W., 79
    popularizing faith rather than religion, 79
business school, 26

Campbell, Joseph, 13–14, 17
    condenses difference, 17
    as storyteller, 14
canon, x
    canonization, viii
Capella, Martianus, 117
Capgrave, John, 121
Capps, Walter, 127
Carter, President Jimmy, 77
Cassirer, Ernst, 48, 111
chance, 6, 114, 121
chemistry, 67
Childs, Brevard S., 46
choice. *See also* religion: typology
    in course design, 23, 96
    of headaches, 55
    political act, 99
Christianity, 79, 100
    early, 112, 115
    Greek Orthodoxy, 35, 59
    in the middle ages, 35
    origins, vii
    problem of evil specific to, 33
    Protestantism, 22, 35, 59
        and public/private politics, 56
    Roman Catholicism, 33, 35
    sin, 33
    Trinitarianism, 32 (*see also* religions: monotheism: history of)
    Unitarianism, 32 (*see also* religions: monotheism: history of)
    universal claims, 66
Church of the Holy Sepulcher, 121
civics, 23
    links to education, 99
    responsible citizen, 43

Claremont College, 88
classics, 6
classification, x, 7n2, 99, 111
    of images of Ganesh vs. Mary, 59, 78
Clifford, James, x
colonialism, British, 56
common sense, 43
comparison, vii, viii, 7, 14, 95, 99, 112, 124, 126. *See also* experimentation
    compare and contrast, 39
    mistaken emphasis on similarity, 39
    none that are natural, 15
    in place of explanation, 50
    with respect to a third/criterion, vii
    with respective to difference, 39
    responsible, 39, 86
    way of handling difference, 39
conclusions
    global vs. modest, 98
Connecticut College, 73
contextualization, 27
contingency. *See* chance
core
    agreement with, 27
    based on faculty consensus, 22
    criticisms of, 21ff.
    designing, 24
    electivity, 21
    general education, 26, 87
    humanities curriculum, 63
    politics of establishing, 22
    repeat in the senior year, 24
    senior seminar, 26
    social science, 14, 87
    taught by junior faculty, 22
    too many Core courses, 22
Cornell University, 5
costs, 54. *See also* questions: costs
culture, x, 11
    as fabricated, x
    memorized, 92
    oral, 92
    synonymous with contact, 92
curiosity, vii, viii, ix, x

Dartmouth College, 103, 112
Darwin, Charles, 9
data, viii
definition, 31–2
  in course design, 88
  definition of, 71
  implies theory, 52
  as limiting, 88
  not descriptions, 71
  not an e.g., 51
  not synonym, 51
  of words in terms of other words, 71
description
  contextual, 112
Dewey, John, 75
Dickens, Charles, 116
dictionaries
  lexical, 89
  specialist, 89
  Webster's not an academic resource, 89
difference, vii, 38, 39, 94
  as complexity, 43
  gives rise to thought, 39
  no natural similarity among religions, 38
  problematics of, 124
  scholars' handling of, 39
digressions, 122
Dionysiacs, 59
Disraeli, Benjamin, 115, 122
dissent, 112
diversity, as educational requirement, 10
  of student population, 81
Doniger, Wendy, 13
  and self appointed guardians, 13
Dubuisson, Daniel, 50
Durkheim Emile, 10, 20, 49, 87, 106
  facts highlighted by student, 65, 106
  as idealist, 48

economics, 56
education. *See also* civics
  area in which faculty should train, 23, 68, 75
  developmental cognition, 27
  effects of technology on, 82
  first vs. second year students, 27
  fourth year students, 27
  highlighting education theory, 26
Eliade, Mircea, ix, 48, 54, 61, 92, 94, 96, 97, 112, 120, 121n14
encounters
  colonial, 60
English Literature, 67, 68
epidemiology, 118
essence, ix
ethnography, x
evil, 33–5
  vs. sin, 33
exempli gratia (e.g.), viii, 49, 114
  on selecting an e.g., 49–50
exotic, 70. *See also* familiar
experience, 105, 120
  experiential learning, 105
  immediate, 30, 121
  mediated (culturally-conditioned), 30, 121
  mystical, 58
  preference for reading over experience, 105
  religious, 79, 121
experimentation (laboratory)
  comparison a version of, 14, 49
  not possible in the human sciences, 14
  process of interfering, 15, 49
  talk a version of, 14, 41
  torture the elements, 14, 49
explanation, 127. *See also* comparison
expert witness, 55

fact vs. opinion, 65, 106
Fairfield University, 29
familiar, 66, 70. *See also* exotic
  familiarization/defamiliarization, 70, 79, 90
Feynman, Richard, 28
fieldwork, 78
Fitzgerald, Timothy, 50

folklore, 87
footnotes, 107. *See also* Smith, Jonathan Z.: reading rules
  authorizing, 122
  long, expository, 122
  look them up, 45
  social science format, 122
Foss, Mark, 6
Foucault, Michel, 14
Frazer, James George, viii, 47, 91, 112, 122, 123
  empirically tested, 47
  footnotes, 124
  The Golden Bough, 48, 122, 123
  as laboratory of comparison, 47
freedom of religion, 105. *See also* choice
  religion as coercion, 105
Freud, Sigmund, 19, 87, 104, 114, 123, 123n19, 123n20
Fujiwara, Satoko, 62–84

Gallagher, Eugene V., 62–84
Ganesh
  described as idol, 59, 78 (*see also* Mary)
gap, 4, 11, 12, 39
Geertz, Clifford, 11, 114, 114n4, 115
gender, x
general education. *See* Core
generalization, 43, 126
  skills of senior faculty, 22
  training in graduate school, 73
Genette, Gérard, 113
Gennep, Arnold van, 96
gerunds, 113, 121
gestures, 59. *See also* ritual
Gibbon, Edward, 122
Golden Rule, the, 17
Gospel Thunder Context, 59
graduate education
  apprenticeship undervalued, 71, 74
  closely tied with undergraduate, 26
  discontinue dissertation, 25

dissertation, 72, 73
excess of PhD graduates/job market issues, 58–9
hired as lectors, 25
keep notebooks, 102
prepare syllabus as part of training, 72
  annotated syllabus, 73
research vs. teaching degree, 74, 80
teaching assistant, 72
teaching first class, 101
  syllabus models/imitation, 101–2
trained to deliver popular lecture, 73
Gray, Hannah, 25

happenstance. *See* chance
Harvard University, 10
  alumni survey, 10
  general education model, 27
Haverford College, 5, 24, 115, 125
  Quaker origins, 6, 24, 46
head hunters, 91
  as quintessential "primitive" for earlier scholars, 91
Hebrew bible, 7
Hegel, G. W. F., 6
  Phenomenology of Mind, 6
hermeneutics of suspicion, 69
Heschel, Abraham, 43
  definition of prophet, 43
Hesiod, 46
Hinduism, 126n24
  Hindu nationalism, 53
  Vedic tradition, 53
Hippocratic oath, 54
hiring
  employment opportunities resulting from Abington v. Schempp, 126
  job ads, 74
  submission of syllabus a requirement, 72–3
history, 5, 42, 68
  historians as negotiator/translator, 5
  of science, 21

history of religions, 46. *See also* study of religion
humanities
  curriculum (*see* Core)
  words the tools, 66
Humboldt, Wilhelm von, 114
humor. *See* jokes
Hunter College Elementary School, 116, 118

iconoclast, viii
imagination, 17, 92, 97, 98
immigration
  greater issue in 2010 in Europe than the US, 56
improvised life, 115. *See also* chance
in-between. *See* gap
incongruity, 39. *See also* surprise
indigenous, ix
ingenuity, 18, 124
interests, ix
International Association for the History of Religions (IAHR), 57, 89
  Marburg Declaration (1960), 89
interpretation, ix, xi, 4, 127. *See also* translation
  of media, 77
  reinterpretation, 53
introductory courses, 63, 74
  history of words, 65
  should be taught by senior faculty, 22, 40
  survey mode, 86, 87
Iranian hostage crisis, 77
Islam, x, 12, 33, 100, 117, 126n24
  European controversy over head covering, 56
  and public/private politics, 56
  Shi'ite, 73

Jainism, 126n24
Jehovah's Witnesses, 78
Jensen, Tim, 62–84

Jesus Christ, 16
joke(s), 6, 18, 20, 29–30, 46, 69, 80, 115
  as parables in class, 21
  vs. sarcasm, 69
  when grass was just what cows ate, 111n2
Jonestown, 49–50, 76
Journal of the American Academy of Religion, 125n23
Journal of the National Association of Biblical Instructors, 125n23
Judaism, 33, 79, 100, 126n24
  early, 112
  purity vs. impurity, 33
Judeo-Christian
  culture, 97
  hyphen the only interesting part, 103
  texts, 97
Jung, Carl G., 120, 121
  individuation, 120n13
juxtaposition, x

Kalimantan religion, 91
  as branch of Hinduism, 92
Koran. *See* Qur'an
Korzybski, Alfred, 121n16

Lang College, 24
language
  92% unconscious, 54
  ambiguous, 13
  foreign vs. native speaker, 43
  no culture-free language, 58
  vs. reality, 30–1
  as second order category, 38
law/law school, 26, 68
Lawson, E. Thomas, 52
Lease, Gary, 8n3, 51
Lehrich, Christopher, 86
Leuba, James, 51
Lévi-Strauss, Claude, 10, 46, 95, 104
  as idealist, 48
liberal arts, 5, 63, 117

Lincoln, Bruce, 96, 99
linguistics, 38
Linnaeus, Carl, 7
literary criticism, x
Livy, 59
local, ix
Luther, Martin, 16

major, college/undergraduate
  abolish majors, 21
  big ideas seminar, 25
  criticism of, 21ff., 28, 99
  double major, 21, 26
  flexibility, 21
  self-designed, 6
  as unimaginative, 6
manure, 5
Marcus, George, x
Marty, Martin, 57
Marx, Karl, 4, 6, 21
  base vs. superstructure, 55
Mary, weeping
  described as icon, 59, 78
mathematics, 68
  as unambiguous, 13
McCauley, Robert N., 52
meaning
  inherent, xi
medical school, 26
middle ground, 33, 37. *See also* gap
  established by education, 36
missionaries, 66, 91
Mitchell, Margaret, 85–6, 108
Momaday, N. Scott, 120
Montaigne, Michel de, 113
moral discourse, 119
mundane, viii, ix
Murray, James, 120
  Oxford English Dictionary, 120
Murray, K. M. Elisabeth, 120
myth, x, 6, 60, 77, 87, 95, 100, 101, 124.
    See also philosophy
  ancestral, 61
  cosmic, 61
  cosmogonic, 66, 70
  endtimes, 100
  Greek, 6
  origins, 17, 100, 125
  structuralist analysis, 46
  thinking with stories, 124
  Tree of Life, 66, 70, 97
    in Genesis, 66, 94
    in Ngaju religion, 66, 92, 94
  universality of, 13

National Association of Bible Instructors (NABI), 125n23
native American, 93
  peyote, 93
negotiation, 4
new criticism, 114
New School, the, 24
New Testament, 6, 47, 115
  and Hellenistic material, 47
  and Jewish material, 47
  as myth, 6, 29, 46
  varieties of, 7
Nietzsche, Friedrich, 114
North American Association for the Study of Religion (NAASR), 113

objective vs. subjective
  change of meaning, 65
old-boy network, 5
Old Testament
  as myth, 46
original/origins. *See also* myth
  absence of, 12
  everyone from somewhere else, 92
  everything a facsimile, 54
  not a choice between original and interpretation, 53
outcomes, 42
  capacities, 42
Oxtoby, Willard, 47

Pearson, Thomas, 62–84
Penner, Hans, 52
Pershing, General John, 118
phenomenology, 58
philology, 66, 116
   false friend, 66
philosophy, 5
   analytic, 6, 17, 46, 64
   Greek, 29
   relationship to Greek myth,
      6, 29, 46
physics, 23, 68, 74
Plato
   Symposium, 24
point of view, 15
   we see through eyeglasses,
      49, 54
   See worldview
political science, 64
PowerPoint, 82
precision, 51
primary text, 90, 91
"primitives" trope, 91
   as original scientists, 91
Princeton University, 10
pristine. *See* original/origins
propaganda, 119
provocation, viii
psychoanalysis, 91

questions
   costs, 44
   out-survive answers, 43–4
   procedure for answering more
      important than answers, 44
Quine, W. V., 124
Qur'an, 7, 14, 17, 87

race, x
Reagan, President Ronald, 77
rectification, 112
redescription, 53, 112
Redfield, James, 9
relativism, 41

religion (singular), 126n24
   basic elements/structures (e.g., myth,
      ritual, etc.), 87, 123, 124
   strategies for dealing with a
      situation, 123
   category made up by scholars, 37, 50
      has no history, 51
      not natural, 41
      not out there, 38
      vs. politics or law, 37
      separation of powers, 37
      word not a thing, 51, 53
   complicated, 36
   deals with difference, 38–9
   definition of, 30–1, 36
   everyday, 59
   vs. faith, 79
   as funny, 4
   as genus, 32
   lived, ix, 78
   material, ix, 60
   narrative power, 32
   on the ground, ix
   popular, 59
   as response to threat, 35
   as subordinate vs. beginner
      category, 31, 52
   superhuman beings, 31
      vs. actors, 52
   supreme being, 32–3
      one and the many, 32
      philosophical vs. religious
         concept, 32
      proof for the existence of, 32–3
      supreme as absolute vs. relative
         term, 32
   as thoughtful, 123
   topic to unteach, 9
   totalizing, 16, 36
   typology
      associative, 90, 93, 97
      matter of personal choice, 90, 93
      imperial, 90, 93
      traditional, 90–1

religion (singular) (*cont.*)
　ethnically constituted, 90
　take advantage of anthropologist's work, 93
religions (plural), 126n24
　alike if translated into English, 34
　and change, 16
　dead, 4, 8, 53
　lack modesty, 16
　as language systems, 38
　monotheism, 32
　　history of, 32
　　limitations of, 33 (*see also* evil)
　none are single issue, 16
　polytheism, 33
　　polemical term, 33
　similarity a product of scholarly interest, 38
　no natural similarity, 38
　species of a genus, 32
religious schools, 67
Ripley, Robert, 122–3
ritual, x, 34, 52, 87, 95, 122, 124. *See also* gesture
　as irrational, 122
　pejorative use of the term, 104
　reduced to text, 60
　rehearsal, 59
　rites of passage, 95
　sacrifice, x, 8
　　economic theory of, 8
　　as metaphor, 8
　　soldiers, 8
Russian-Turkish War, 116n6
Ryle, Gilbert, 124

Sandmel, Samuel, 47
Sartre, Jean-Paul, 120
Schärer, Hans, 66n1, 91, 95
　summary of myth, 95
science(s), natural, 11, 68, 86
　built-in modesty, 36
secularism
　in England, 56
　in France, 56
　in the US, 56
self-conscious scholarship, viii, xii, 41, 67, 75
　as primary expertise, ix
seminars
　young person's game, 9
sex education, 118
　What Fathers Should Tell Their Sons, 118
　What Mothers Should Tell Their Daughters, 118
signification
　theory of, xii
similarity
　college students drawn to it, 94
sincerity, 113
single quotation marks (scare quotes), 51
Sinhababu, Supriya, 3–28
Smith, Elaine, xiii, 3, 4, 17, 28, 45, 75, 80, 84, 108, 121
Smith, Jonathan Z.
　agrostology, 5, 7, 111, 117n7
　autodidact, 119, 127
　Bachelor of Divinity (BD), 30, 46, 47, 112
　books by
　　Drudgery Divine, viii, 7n2, 86
　　Imagining Religion, viiin1, viii, ix, 7n2, 71, 86
　　"there is no data for religion," viii, 71 (*see* religion: category made up by scholars)
　　Map is Not Territory, 7n2, 86, 121n16
　　On Teaching Religion, 86, 101
　　Relating Religion, 7n2, 86, 115, 119n11
　　To Take Place, 86
　cane, 18
　　liberated from Great Smoky Mountain National Park, 19
　　made by uncle, 19
　　rhododendron, 18

classroom assessments
   designated discussant, 83, 107
   dislike of senior projects, 25
   final essays, 67, 105
   grading for grammar, 75
   topics given not chosen, 67
   portfolios, 25
   reading reports, 64, 67
   re-reading/revising earlier essays, 24, 67, 89
   student books/journals, 20, 64, 105
   student feedback at end of class, 83, 107
   weekly writing, 98, 105
computers, xiii, 3, 99, 122
   alienation, critique of, 4
   automation, critique of, 122
   no email, 45
courses
   Bibles in Western Civilization, 7, 87
   honors papers, 88
   Introduction to the New Testament, 88
   Introduction to Religion, 88
   not including theory, 95–6
   shortcoming of excluding theology, 100
   Introduction to Religious Studies, 102–3
   The Judeo-Christian Tradition, 103
   studying the hyphen, 103
   reading courses, 88, 118
   Religions in Western Civilization, 88
   Self, Culture, and Society, 10
   social science core, 42
   on telephone book, 42
   used in exam, 59
critical turn in the study of religion, and, xi
criticisms of, ix
Dean of the College, 23, 26, 48
definition of professor, 43

dissertation
   as advisor, 88
   by, viii, 47, 122n18, 124
distrust of technology/luddite moments, 4, 21, 58 (*see* Vietnam War)
   black box, 45
essayist, xi, 86
essays
   "Acknowledgments: Morphology and History in Mircea Eliade's *Patterns in Comparative Religions* (1949–1999)," parts 1 and 2, 7n2
   "The Bare Facts of Ritual," 49n4
   "The Devil in Mr. Jones," 49n4, 76
   "The Introductory Course: Less is Better," 96n6
   "Epilogue: The 'End' of Comparison," 7n2
   "Map is Not Territory," 121n16
   "The Necessary Lie," 19–20, 21, 23, 28
   not intended for publication, 19
   "On Comparison," 7n2
   "Religious Studies: Whither (wither) and Why?" 86
   "When the Chips are Down," 5n1, 7n2, 115, 119n11, 121, 124n21
exorcised (almost), 79
handwritten essays, 3
   as idealist, 48, 120
   and internet, 19
garden, 8
honors college
   study a single sentence, 118
love of reading, 115–16, 119
   dictionaries, 116
   library vs. travel, 121
   mediated vs. immediate experience, 121
memory, 119
method
   double archaeology, 49

Smith, Jonathan Z. (*cont.*)
  persistent preoccupations, 7n2, 115, 124n21
  philosophy major, 6, 46, 115, 123
  prefers map over territory, 121
  president of
    North American Association for the Study of Religion (1996–2002), 113, 125n23
    Society of Biblical Literature (2008), 113, 125n23
  publications, tested in the classroom, 61
  ratemyprofessor.com, 18
  reading rules, 58, 119, 119n11
  retirement, 16
  senior theses, 46
  smoking, 3, 6, 28
    17 feet from an entrance ordinance, 28
    smoking break for students to write, 71, 89
  syllabus, 86ff.
    as academic writing, 87
    descriptive vs. argumentative, 87
    institutional requirements, 103
    odd genre, 102
    owning ones own, 102, 103
    rarely publishes, 64
    vs. reading list, 87, 96–7
    as site of choice, 87
    title as object of interrogation, 88
    topic of first class, 41
    unable to teach someone else's, 63, 88, 102
  taught at public vs. private schools, 47
  teaching, 8, 64
    Aha! moments, 40
    anthologies, 102
    attending student functions, 81
    booby traps/time bombs, 66, 90–2
    discussion-based classes, 107
    emphasize writing, 63
    experienced teachers must recover their insecurity, 102
    first class definitions of religion, 71, 89
    haphazard business, 99
    improvisation, 72
    incomplete sentences, 18
    instigate conversation, 98
    interesting gossip, 99
    place of criticism in class, 83
    portfolio, 73
    presentation styles, 72
    problem-solving, 72
    problem-based learning, 77
    questions on last day, 69 (*see also* question: out-survive answers)
    reading and writing skills interconnected, 106
    team teaching, 104
    textbooks, 102
    throw away notes at end of class, 84
    using newspapers in class, 76, 77–8
      Iranian hostage crisis e.g., 77
    using summaries of myths, 95
    wrinkles on brows, 69
    writing, 72
  telephones, and, xiii, 3, 45
    cell phone an abomination, 3
  typewriters, and, 4
  vegetarian, 29, 48
    youthful Buddhist rationale for, 29
  writing in library books a mortal sin, 119
  youthful rewriting of the biblical narratives, 123
Smith Wilfred Cantwell, 12
  authorized participants, 12
  insider is best informed, 53
so what? question, the vii
Society of Biblical Literature (SBL), 113, 125n23
sociology, 59
  of religion, 78

sound bites, scholarship as, 57
specialization, 22, 27. *See also* generalization
Spiro, Melford, 31, 52
spontaneity, 107
statistics, 119
Sterne, Laurence, 122
study of religion. *See also* Supreme Court of the United States: Abington v. Schempp
  absence as a subject in US high schools, 67
  challenges for the future, 58–9, 127
  studies of the non-verbal, 59, 78
  cognitive science and, 50
  as criticism of multiple readings vs. quest for originals, 54
  current issues in the US field, 57–8
    cognitive science of religion, 58
    critical theory of religion, 57
    decline in primary source language expertise, 57
  as overcorrection, 57
    increased interest in religion rather than religions, 57
    increased internationalization, 57–8
  in Denmark, 65, 68, 73, 78
    didactics of religious education, 73
    preparing school teachers, 68
  exporting terms as if they are general, 34
  finding sense in religion, 30, 101
  fun field of study, 70
    having fun vs. making fun of, 70
  history of the study of religion, 65
  increase in number of US departments post-1963, 55, 126
  largely unrealized, 126
  legitimacy, 31
  no peculiar pedagogy, 63
  presupposes some distance, 104
  as primary text, 39, 87
  in public university economic opportunity, 55
  Religionswissenschaft, 89
  as science of religion, 50
  species vs. genera, 126
  vs. theology, 30–1
    tactical distinction, 29
  tourist vs. convert, 11
  zoo model of the study of religion, 10, 11
Sumerian Kesh Temple Hymn, 120
Supreme Court of the United States
  Abington v. Schempp (1963), 47, 55, 90n2, 115, 125, 125n22
    teaching about religion vs teaching of religion, 125
    conception of religion as personal choice, 94 (*see also* religion: typology)
    diversity quotas vs. targets, 10
surprise (evidenced by laughter). *See also* incongruity
  as way to select an e.g., 49

Taves, Ann, 111–13, 114
taxonomy, 7, 7n2
  of educational objectives, 76
teaching
  class size, 80
  office hours, 80
  as political act, 55, 99
  role of student's faith commitment, 63, 64, 79
  and students' predispositions, 97
television
  effect on awareness of cultural different, 36–7
theodicy. *See* evil
theory
  considered an avocation, 126
  lack of training in, 127
  second order discourse, 126–7
  study of religion largely a parasitic field, 60

Toleration Act (1689), 56. *See* secularism: in England
  breakdown today, 56
  private freedom exchanged for public conformity, 56
Toulmin, Stephen, 127
tradition, 98, 100
  absorption of novelty, 100
  comprised of multiple interpretations, 98
translation, xi, 12, 34, 37, 38, 43, 45, 66, 126
  changes things, 12
  different from interpretation, 50
  paraphrase/repletion inadequate, 12
Turner, Victor, 104
Tylor, E. B., 98

undergraduate education. *See also* Core
  and citizenship, 43
  main goal is not preparation for graduate school, 40
  over-professionalized, 67
  training to read, write, argue, 40, 41, 63
unique, vii, ix
University of California, Berkeley, 118
University of California, Santa Barbara, 20, 48, 63, 81, 88, 118, 127n26
  Honors College, 118
University of Chicago, 76, 79, 80, 81, 111
  School of Continuing Education, 117

University of Chicago College, 23, 48, 112, 117
University of Chicago Divinity School, 48, 75, 101, 112
  Craft of Teaching Seminar, 85ff.
  courtesy appointment, 48
University of Michigan, 10
Ur, 100

Vietnam War, 21. *See* Smith, Jonathan Z.: distrust of technology
  selective service, 21

Wellesley College, 25
Wiggins, Jim, 126
Wikipedia
  as source of authority in classes, 82
"wild-man of Borneo" trope, 91
wink, 60. *See also* gesture; ritual
worldview, 15

Yale University
  Divinity School, 6, 29, 46, 112, 115
  established Department of Religion outside Divinity, 47
  Smith first History of Religions PhD, 115, 125
  Smith moves from Divinity, 47, 124
  Smith second non-Christian to earn a BD at Yale, 47

www.ingramcontent.com/pod-product-compliance
Ingram Content Group UK Ltd.
Pitfield, Milton Keynes, MK11 3LW, UK
UKHW021252180426

11946UKWH00004B/99

9 780190 879082